Entertainment WEEKLY

YEARBOOK 2000

TABLE OF
CONTENTS

American Beauty's Wes Bentley, TV's Chris Meloni, Julia Stiles, *The Sixth Sense*'s Haley Joel Osment, *The Matrix*'s Carrie-Anne Moss, the hosts of *The Man Show*, *Providence*'s Melina Kanakaredes, the cast of the teen hit *American Pie*, pop's Christina Aguilera, and author Melissa Bank.

The sexy cast of *Sex and the City*, Molly Shannon, Joan Cusack, Jon Stewart, the Backstreet Boys, Cher, Janet McTeer, Margaret Cho, Rene Russo, Russell Crowe, Mark Wahlberg, *South Park* on the big screen, and others.

The View lost Debbie, *ER* lost George, and *Saving Private Ryan* lost Oscar; David Blaine went underground; and Monica Lewinsky came out and told all; mobsters were hot; Springsteen came back; Tom and Nicole sizzled...then fizzled; the three-day Woodstock festival sparked controversy; and so much more.

On the set, behind the scenes, plus portraits.

The women who got the fashion thing right this year.

Fond farewells to Stanley Kubrick, George C. Scott, Gene Siskel, Joe DiMaggio, Mel Tormé, and others.

YEARBOOK 2000 STAFF
EDITOR Cynthia A. Grisolia
ART DIRECTOR Joe Kimberling
PICTURE EDITOR Alice H. Babcock

DEPUTY EDITOR Joe Neumaier
SENIOR WRITERS Betty Cortina, Scott Brown
ASSOCIATE EDITOR Julie Haire
ASSISTANT PICTURE EDITOR Luciana Chang
REPORTERS Julia Dahl, Emily Drabinski,
Nicholas Fonseca, Rebecca Hirschfield,
Riki S. Markowitz, Joshua Rich, Adam Winer
EDITORIAL PRODUCTION MANAGER John K. Horsky
COPY CHIEF Ben Spier
DEPUTY COPY CHIEF David Penick
COPY EDITORS Roseann Marulli, Michelle Patient
SPECIAL THANKS TO The EW Library Staff

TIME INC. HOME ENTERTAINMENT
PRESIDENT Stuart Hotchkiss
EXECUTIVE DIRECTOR, BRANDED BUSINESSES
David Arfine
EXECUTIVE DIRECTOR, NONBRANDED BUSINESSES
Alicia Longobardo
EXECUTIVE DIRECTOR, TIME INC. BRAND LICENSING
Risa Turken
DIRECTOR, MARKETING SERVICES Michael Barrett
DIRECTOR, RETAIL & SPECIAL SALES Tom Mifsud
ASSOCIATE DIRECTORS Roberta Harris,
Kenneth Maehlum
PRODUCT MANAGERS Andre Okolowitz,
Niki Viswanathan, Daria Rachsc
ASSOCIATE PRODUCT MANAGERS Dennis Sheehan,
Meredith Shelley, Bill Totten, Lauren Zaslansky
ASSISTANT PRODUCT MANAGERS Victoria Alfonso,
Jennifer Dowell, Ann Gillespie
LICENSING MANAGER JoAnna West
ASSOCIATE LICENSING MANAGER Regina Feiler
ASSOCIATE MANAGER, RETAIL & NEW MARKETS
Bozena Szwagulinski
EDITORIAL OPERATIONS DIRECTOR John Calvano
BOOK PRODUCTION MANAGER Jessica McGrath
ASSISTANT BOOK PRODUCTION MANAGER
Jonathan Polsky
BOOK PRODUCTION COORDINATOR Kristen Lizzi
FULFILLMENT MANAGER Richard Perez
ASSISTANT FULFILLMENT MANAGER Tara Schimming
FINANCIAL DIRECTOR Tricia Griffin
FINANCIAL MANAGER Robert Dente
ASSOCIATE FINANCIAL MANAGER Steven Sandonato
EXECUTIVE ASSISTANT Mary Jane Rigoroso
SPECIAL THANKS TO Emily Rabin, Jennifer Bomhoff,
Alison Ehrmann

ISBN: 1-883013-86-0
ISSN: 1097-5705

We welcome your comments and suggestions about Entertainment
Weekly Books. Please write to us at ENTERTAINMENT WEEKLY
Book Editors, P.O. Box 11016, Des Moines, IA 50336-1016

If you would like to order any of our Hardcover Collector Edition
Books, please call us at 1-800-327-6388 (Monday through Friday,
7 a.m.–6 p.m., Central Time).

Entertainment WEEKLY

EDITOR IN CHIEF: Norman Pearlstine
EDITORIAL DIRECTOR: Henry Muller

CHAIRMAN, CEO: Don Logan
EXECUTIVE VICE PRESIDENTS: Richard Atkinson, Elizabeth Valk Long, Jim Nelson

MANAGING EDITOR: James W. Seymore Jr.
EXECUTIVE EDITORS: Peter Bonventre, Richard Sanders
ASSISTANT MANAGING EDITORS: Mark Harris, Maggie Murphy, Mary Kaye Schilling
DESIGN DIRECTOR: Geraldine Hessler **PHOTOGRAPHY DIRECTOR:** Sarah Rozen **L.A. BUREAU CHIEF:** Cable Neuhaus
SENIOR EDITORS: Doug Brod, Jamie Bufalino, Ty Burr, Jess Cagle, Tina Jordan, John McAlley
DIRECTOR OF RESEARCH SERVICES: Annabel Bentley **SPECIAL PROJECTS EDITOR:** Cynthia A. Grisolia
EDITORIAL MANAGER: Louis Vogel **STAFF EDITORS:** Kristen Baldwin, Marc Bernardin, Dulcy Israel, A. J. Jacobs **CRITIC-AT-LARGE:** Ken Tucker
CRITICS: David Browne, Bruce Fretts, Owen Gleiberman, Lisa Schwarzbaum **WRITER-AT-LARGE:** Benjamin Svetkey
SENIOR WRITERS: Rebecca Ascher-Walsh, Betty Cortina, Steve Daly, Jeff Gordinier, David Hochman,
Christopher Nashawaty, Noah Robischon, Chris Willman
SENIOR ASSOCIATE EDITORS: Eileen Clarke, Tracy A. Walsh **ASSOCIATE EDITORS:** Wook Kim, Alice King,
Joe Neumaier, Bianca Perlman, Jessica Shaw (L.A.), William Stevenson, Mitchell Vinicor, Fan Wong
STAFF WRITERS: Mike Flaherty, Jeff Jensen, Dave Karger, Lynette Rice, Dalton Ross, Tom Sinclair, Dan Snierson
CORRESPONDENTS: Rob Brunner, Daniel Fierman, Tricia Johnson, Troy Patterson, Corey Takahashi
SENIOR BROADCAST CORRESPONDENT: Lisa Karlin
DESIGN ART DIRECTOR: John Walker **MANAGING ART DIRECTOR:** Joe Kimberling
ASSISTANT ART DIRECTORS: Jennifer Procopio, Ellene Standke, Liliane Vilmenay **DESIGNERS:** Jennie Chang, Edith L. Gutierrez
IMAGING TECHNICIAN: Susan Van Over **ASSISTANT:** Elizabeth M. Lastique
PICTURES PICTURE EDITOR: Denise Sfraga **WEST COAST PICTURE EDITOR:** Michael Kochman **ASSOCIATE PICTURE EDITOR:** Alice H. Babcock
ASSISTANT PICTURE EDITORS: Helena V. Ashton, Richard B. Maltz, Suzanne Regan, Michele Romero, Freyda C. Tavin
PICTURE COORDINATOR: Luciana Chang **ASSISTANT:** L. Michelle Dougherty
RESEARCH SERVICES DEPUTY: Tim Purtell **SENIOR REPORTER:** Beth Johnson
REPORTERS: Allyssa Lee, Leslie Marable, Joshua Rich, Erin Richter, Nancy Sidewater, Daneet Steffens, Lori L. Tharps
INFORMATION CENTER MANAGER: Rachel Sapienza **DEPUTY:** Stacie Fenster **SENIOR ASSOCIATE:** Sean O'Heir **ASSOCIATE:** Alexandria Carrion
COPY COPY CHIEF: Ben Spier **DEPUTY COPY CHIEF:** David Penick
EDITORIAL ASSISTANTS Clarissa Cruz, Gillian Flynn, Will Lee, Ann Limpert, Leonard McCants, Laura Morgan, Brian M. Raftery
ADMINISTRATION ASSISTANT TO THE MANAGING EDITOR: Rita Silverstein **STAFF:** Carole Willcocks
EW.COM EXECUTIVE EDITOR: Michael Small **EDITOR:** Mark Bautz **ART DIRECTOR:** Alexander Knowlton **SENIOR TECHNOLOGIST:** Jason Lane
SENIOR PRODUCER: Heather White **PRODUCTION DEVELOPER:** Chris Sizemore **STAFF WRITERS:** Liane Bonin, Josh Wolk
CORRESPONDENT: Craig Seymour **ASSISTANT ART DIRECTOR:** Stella Anastasia **MULTIMEDIA PRODUCER:** Matthew Kronsberg
ASSOCIATE EDITOR: Angie Argabrite **ASSOCIATE PRODUCER:** Rachel Lovinger
ASSISTANT PICTURE EDITOR: Connie Yu **EDITORIAL ASSISTANT:** Sandra P. Angulo
PRODUCTION MAKEUP MANAGER: Robin Kaplan **OPERATIONS MANAGER:** Karen S. Doyle
AD PRODUCTION SUPERVISOR: Ann Griffith O'Connor **ASSISTANT MAKEUP MANAGERS:** Shell Azar, Don Gordon
ASSISTANT OPERATIONS MANAGER: Nicol D. DeVito **PRODUCTION COORDINATORS:** Jacklyn Bruce, Amy J. Houston, Karen E. Sharp
IMAGING AND MAGAZINE TECHNOLOGIES DIRECTOR: Jeffrey Cherins **MANAGERS:** Paul Bodley Jr., Melanie Wertz
ASSISTANT MANAGER: Jason Schlau **SENIOR PRODUCTION ASSOCIATES:** Ray Battaglino, George L. Beke, Evan J. Dong, John Goodman,
Michael R. Hargreaves, John K. Horsky, Robert D. Kennedy, Bill Lazzarotti, Eileen M. O'Sullivan, Tom Roemlein, David Serrano, George
Sumerak, Daniel C. Thompson **DESKTOP SUPPORT ANALYSTS:** Alfredo Matos, Godwin Mensah, Jeff Walthers
CONTRIBUTORS Judith I. Brennan, Pat H. Broeske, Caren Weiner Campbell, Heidi Siegmund Cuda, Mike D'Angelo,
Tom De Haven, Vanessa V. Friedman, Megan Harlan, L.S. Klepp, Gene Lyons, Lois Alter Mark, Margot Mifflin, Jim Mullen,
Alanna Nash, Degen Pener, Michael Sauter, Stephen Schaefer, Zack Stentz, Josh Young

PRESIDENT: John Squires
PUBLISHER: Michael J. Kelly
VICE PRESIDENT, CONSUMER MARKETING: Monica Ray
VICE PRESIDENT, GENERAL MANAGER: Cathy O'Brien
DIRECTOR OF PRODUCTION & TECHNOLOGY: Carol A. Mazzarella
ASSOCIATE PUBLISHER: David S. Morris
VICE PRESIDENT, MARKETING & PROMOTION: Fred O. Nelson
DIRECTOR OF PUBLIC RELATIONS & COMMUNICATIONS: Sandy W. Drayton
DIRECTOR OF EW.COM: William J. Stutzman
CONSUMER MARKETING: Tammy Laspalakis (Assistant Director); Matthew T. Chang, Gary Foodim, Timothy M. Smith, Holley Vantrease,
Vincent M. Vero (Managers); Rit Chatterjee, Eleanor Hong, Amy G. Kapper; Stephanie Solomon, Wynne Wong; Taleen Gergerian
ADVERTISING SALES: Headquarters: Thomas A. Morrissy (Eastern Manager); Carole S. Harnoff (Classified Sales Manager); Dylan Parks;
Ellen Jacobson, Felice Pilchik **ATLANTA:** Andrew M. Davis (Manager); Mara Masso **CHICAGO:** Eileen Cavanaugh (Midwest Manager);
Jennifer Plepel **DETROIT:** Danielle Morris (Manager); Patricia H. Dugan, Stephen C. Larson (Sales Representatives); Maryanne Murawski
LOS ANGELES: Linda A. Villani (Manager); Kimberly Allen (Associate Manager); Matthew J. Sganga (Sales Representative);
Melinda A. Carson, Jill Doohen **NEW YORK:** Cara B. Bernstein, Julie Chang, Raymond T. Chelstowski, Jodi H. Cohen, Melissa J. Nadler,
Julie R. Schoenberg, Suzanne Speichinger (Sales Representatives); Tomika L. Anderson, Tracy S. Gardner, Kevin R. Sitson
SAN FRANCISCO: Jacque Lapsey (Manager); Christine Connolly (Sales Representative); Alison D. Osborne **DALLAS:** Jo Neese,
Tammy Stilling (Kelly/Tremblay & Company)
MARKETING & PROMOTION: Rose Bleszcz, Gail L. Chen, Karen Gottschalk, Kathleen A. Moore,
Elizabeth A. Ronan (Directors); Steven T. Porter; Kelly Kim, Derek Milsted, Stephanie Miness (Managers); Sheila M. Kelly, Mel Sanchez,
Jacqueline L. Stiles, Deborah White, Jenny Wong
PUBLIC RELATIONS: Jason T. Averett
FINANCE & ADMINISTRATION: FINANCE: Stephanie B. Torre (Director); Sherry W. Burns; Beverly Ivens, Jane L. Koty, Richard J. Schexnider;
Suzanne Shakter; Vivian Adamakos, Miriam T. Fernando
ADMINISTRATION: Ilissa R. Sternlicht (Manager); Carolyn L. Burnett, Sandie Baum, Sheila Drouet
LEGAL: Amy Glickman

TIME INC.
EXECUTIVE EDITORS: Joëlle Attinger, José M. Ferrer III
DEVELOPMENT EDITOR: Jacob Young **EDITORS-AT-LARGE:** Donald L. Barlett, Susan Casey, Steve Lopez, Steven M. Lovelady, Daniel Okrent,
Roger Rosenblatt, Danyel Smith, James B. Steele **TIME INC. EDITORIAL SERVICES:** Sheldon Czapnik (Director);
Claude Boral (General Manager); Thomas E. Hubbard (Photo Lab); Lany Walden McDonald (Research Center); Beth Bencini Iskander,
Kathi Doak (Picture Collection); Thomas Smith (Technology)
TIME INC. EDITORIAL TECHNOLOGY: Paul Zazzera (Vice President); Damien Creavin (Director)

It's all about The Moment. That instant when creativity, talent, the perfect part (or the perfect song), and maybe a little magic strike the right performer at just the right time. The result? For the celebrated dozen on the following pages, it's a place on EW's honor roll of Entertainers of the Year. Some of our chosen ones are familiar faces: pretty woman Julia Roberts, who sparkled in not one but two smash hits this summer, *Notting Hill* and *Runaway Bride*; '70s Latin-flavored rock king Carlos Santana, who resisted the typical nostalgia pull and instead released a timeless album, *Supernatural*; Denzel Washington, who collected audiences for *The Bone Collector* and whipped up awards buzz with *The Hurri-*

THE
ENTERTAINERS

cane; and David Chase, who toiled in television for more than two decades before HBO gambled on his crime-family-values saga, *The Sopranos*—and turned the longtime writer-producer into a Made Man. Of course, there are also the year's fresh faces—like bubblegum baby Britney Spears, *Being John Malkovich*'s head cheese Spike Jonze, imaginative *Harry Potter* authoress J. K. Rowling, and the novice filmmakers and actors behind *The Blair Witch Project*, who found a multimillion-dollar response to the question, If a thriller is made for no money in the woods, will anyone go see it? (The answer: *Oh, yeah.*) As it turns out, the No. 1 spot in this year's entertainment universe belongs to a performer who was both a familiar face to some and a newcomer to others. And that would be....

RICKY MARTIN

Ricky Martin turned 28 years old on Christmas Eve—fitting for a man who could change his name to the Second Coming without much argument. Twelve months ago most of us hadn't heard of this Puerto Rican pop sensation—though he was already a superstar overseas. Then in February, Martin added America to his international conquests with his who's-that-boy? performance of "La Copa de la Vida" during the Grammys. As of right now, his first English-language album, *Ricky Martin*, has sold more than 6 million copies and spawned three hit singles, including the inescapable "Livin' la Vida Loca." "It's been crazy," says Martin, who began his showbiz journey 16 years ago with Menudo before moving to roles on *General Hospital* and in Broadway's *Les Misérables*. "I've been working nonstop since I was 12, and intensely for the last three years at least." It shows: Lounging in a hotel suite before one of his 24 sold-out concerts, his voice is deceptively soft. But an hour later, when he takes to the stage, he shakes his bon-bon as if the future of humanity depended on it. Martin opens the show by invoking the name of Venezuelan liberator Simón Bolívar: "One of his dreams was to unite the Americas," Martin tells his audience, "and we're going to do some of that tonight." And this promise, above all else, is why Ricky Martin must hold the title of Entertainer of the Year, 1999. Let it never be said that Martin pioneered a Latin-music invasion. While he did ignite the current boom (see also Jennifer Lopez, Enrique Iglesias, Marc Anthony, etc.), his particular fusion of mambo, salsa, and pop-rock has been done before. What sets Martin apart is his heartfelt mission: to shatter stereotypes of Latinos. "Whatever I have to do to unite Latin America with the rest of the world, well, let's go for it," he says. So be it. The beautiful thing about Martin is his driving ambition to share the strength of his faith and the love of his homeland. Oh sure, his music is easy on the ears, and he's easy on the eyes. But isn't it lovely that on the eve of a new millennium, one step closer to tranquillity or oblivion, we've reached for a shaft of light? —*Jess Cagle*

DAVID
CHASE

Some writers see it coming when they forge a culture-shaking hit. Not David Chase. He remembers sitting on the set of the HBO series *The Sopranos* saying "Who the hell is going to watch this?" More than audience indifference, Chase dreaded a critical drubbing. "I was sure they were gonna go, 'Another Mafia thing? Kill it!'" He pantomimes raising a rifle—"Pull!"—then squeezes an imaginary trigger: "Ka*BOOM*!" But *The Sopranos* proved a target only for accolades: The 13-episode series pulled in as many as 10 million viewers a week, was dubbed a virtual masterpiece by pundits, and scored 16 Emmy nominations—nailing 4, including a cowriting statuette for Chase. The irony is that if Chase's inspired update of the milieus mined in *The Godfather* and *GoodFellas* had been picked up by Fox TV, for which it was developed in the mid-'90s, it might well have lost its soul. "There's been a lot of talk about how everybody at Fox and a couple other networks are so sorry they didn't say yes," he says. "That's not really true. If Fox had said yes, everybody would have been unhappy.... This turned out to be a show that you could not put anywhere but pay cable." Beyond the obvious sex and violence reasons, there's rhythm. Broadcast TV requires crescendos every 12 minutes or so; but the saga of Tony Soprano (James Gandolfini), a suburban New Jersey crime boss laid low by anxiety attacks, hinges on understatement, indirection, and denial. "Network TV is all about people saying *exactly* what's on their minds," says Chase. "This show is about people *not* saying what's on their minds." Though he works with a stable of writers, producers, and directors, Chase is the final arbiter of casting, editing, and scoring. The cast and crew call him "the master cylinder," and they're confident he'll keep the spark going in subsequent seasons, even if Chase has his doubts. "If it isn't as good, it just won't be as good," he shrugs. For all the praise, Chase still hears the cry he heard before everything turned golden. *Pull! —Steve Daly/Photograph by Dana Lixenberg*

THE BLAIR
WITCH
PROJECT

One of the most fascinating bits of *The Blair Witch Project* myth has nothing to do with the movie's plot—it's deciphering whether the biggest indie success story to date is the work of inspired wunderkinds or a stroke of marketing genius. Critics say "the film was a fluke, that it did business because of the website," says Eduardo Sanchez, 31, who directed the pseudodocumentary with Daniel Myrick, 36. "People are saying…'but can they make a normal film?'" One studio exec even asked if they knew how to write a straightforward script. Granted, most of *Blair* is improvised, but Sanchez and Myrick weren't just stumbling through the Maryland woods. The Florida film-school pals auditioned actors for a year before picking unknowns Heather Donahue, Joshua Leonard, and Michael Williams. And breaking the fright formula—shiny knives, bloody flesh, helpless babes—can't be underrated, either. Sanchez and Myrick sensed movie-goers' ennui with gore and special effects and went the opposite way. The payoff could have been ruined with a glitzy trailer, but Artisan Entertainment, *Blair*'s distributor, followed the film's wooded path, and went with minimalism: two sentences, a voiceover, half a face, and a web address. The site was arguably the most brilliant stroke; instead of the usual PR repository, Artisan passed *Blair* off as a real documentary. The site helped *Blair* become one of the most profitable films in history (it cost under $100,000 and has earned over $210 million worldwide). Whether Sanchez and Myrick are inspired mavericks or just plain lucky will be revealed soon: In January, they plan to shoot a trailer for their next film, the comedy *Heart of Love.* —*Noah Robischon/Photograph by Moshe Brakha*

LEONARD   DONAHUE   WILLIAMS

BRITNEY
SPEARS

When Britney Spears addresses the guy she hopes will hit her one more time (with the truth, not his fist), she calls him her "baby" in a growly moan that would do a veteran soul singer proud. "Oh, *bay*-buh, *bay*-buh" is her refrain, and that throaty purr, combined with the pert video that was all over MTV like chocolate on a Ding Dong, turned the 18-year-old Spears into an end-of-century sex kitten who'd humble Humbert Humbert. Not that there's anything wrong with that, since Spears bypasses Nympho-ville and zooms straight into the Mall-lands of America, where her public appearances make prepubescent fans scream with innocent delight. What the little girls in Spears' sphere get is that their idol is one confident role model who's chosen her own influences well: a bit of Janet Jackson in her dance moves, a smidgen of Mariah Carey's sultry sassiness, some Stevie Wonder in her croon, and, behind the scenes, Backstreet Boys mentor Max Martin cowriting and co-producing unshakable pop hits. Spears' '99 debut, …*Baby One More Time*, has sold more than 9 million copies, and her non-mall stadium tours were sellout hormonal fits. Spears knows where she's coming from, artistically speaking. She sees her art through the mists of ancient pop history: "There was a period when R&B was really strong. You didn't hear any pop. It was like New Kids on the Block, and then all of a sudden it just went away." Britney, on the heels of the Backstreet Boys, helped bring pop back. And, on the much higher heels of the Spice Girls, she's taken girl power to the next level. Spears has tapped into hip-hop's free-flowing sensuality without scaring off kids or their 'rents, duplicating moves that are funky but not so freaky they can't be reproduced by little girls in front of their mirrors. "My audience looks at me like a girlfriend," says Spears. "That's how I was trying to portray it on stage. Instead of being, like, 'I've got a man and duh-duh-duh.' I didn't want the jealousy thing." Someday, Britney, you'll be old enough to sing comfortably about how you "got a man," but in the meantime, trust us: "Oh, *bay*-buh, *bay*-huh" is a pop mantra as good as anyone needs right now. —*Ken Tucker*

We can't say they didn't warn us. In January, the World Wrestling Federation aired its first Super Bowl commercial: a 30-second spot that showed WWF headbangers at the firm's Stamford, Conn., headquarters, dryly extolling its integrity and wholesomeness as scenes of wanton carnage unfolded in the background. The final shot: A body blasts through a window as bemused WWF chairman Vince McMahon turns to the camera and asks, "Get it?" Apparently, we did. If wrestling was everywhere in '99, it's thanks to the WWF. McMahon's baby not only scaled new ratings heights, it expanded its reach to network with UPN's *WWF Smackdown!* More opera than soap opera, the WWF's productions have evolved into not just unabashed celebrations of id but some of the year's funniest TV—thanks to its fearless leader. Businessman, carny, auteur, and evil genius, McMahon, 54, has become a bona fide TV star, the John Forsythe of this multimedia dynasty. "Other than being a scientist who finds a cure for some disease," says McMahon, "the next best thing in life is entertaining the public." In October, to cap the federation's stunning success—and finance new ones—McMahon took the family business (worth an estimated $1.4 billion) public. He wasn't the only one cashing in. Among the WWF's stable of superstars (don't call them wrestlers), The Rock reigned supreme. In a world where loudmouthed hyperbole is the norm, Duane Johnson, 27, actually lived up to his self-bestowed title as "the most electrifying man in sports entertainment." A swaggering antihero with an ego to match his biceps, The Rock laid the smackdown on his opponents in the ring and on the mike. Not that controversy hasn't attended its triumphs. The death of wrestler Owen Hart in a rigging accident and recent advertiser defections (thanks, in part, to condemnation by a parents' advocacy group) should make 2000 more challenging. But "Vinnie Mac" is a survivor, and if he's got anything to say about it, professional wrestling is here to stay. Besides, anything that can raise the rancor of religious fundamentalists and the cultural elite must be doing something right. —*Mike Flaherty/Photograph by Moshe Brakha*

THE
WWF

THE ROCK AND McMAHON

6

J.K. ROWLING

The historical record will show that at the wired end of our weird century, in the surge of digital this and dot-com that and the reign of the moving image, a mammoth cult sprang up around a series of children's books. The first three novels written by J.K. Rowling—the first of seven volumes following a boy named Harry Potter to graduation from the Hogwarts School of Witchcraft and Wizardry—own the top three spots on the *New York Times* hardcover fiction best-seller list. There are now 17.4 million copies of her books in print. At readings this year, tykes squealed with hysteria while Rowling signed, say, 900 books at a stretch. Some witch-hunting types want Harry out of schoolrooms; some rival authors want him banished to a children's best-seller list. The movie rights for the first two novels, *Harry Potter and the Sorcerer's Stone* and *Harry Potter and the Chamber of Secrets*, sold to Warner Bros., and Steven Spielberg is rumored to be interested. All in all, it's a publishing frenzy without precedent. "We're living in a world where imagination is succumbing to rationality and technology," says Jack Zipes, a University of Minnesota professor and an expert on fairy tales, "and here's a [wizard] as the last defender of the imagination." Orphaned when the forces of the Dark Lord Voldemort struck down his enchanting parents, Harry Potter grows up in the dreary home of his aunt and uncle, who are Muggles (mortals). Each book advances Harry through another year at Hogwarts, the site of fierce battles against Evil and fiercer boarding-school high jinks. "It's not just an exaggerated fairy tale or a fantasy," says Arthur Levine, who bought Harry's U.S. rights for his self-named imprint at Scholastic. "The novel speaks to a part of the human condition, which is that we all sometimes feel like we're actors in a bad script and want to escape." When Joanne Rowling, 34, started *Stone*, she was a single mom living on the dole in Scotland. The idea of Harry came to her on a train. "She wasn't trying to write a book for children," says Emma Matthewson, her editor at England's Bloomsbury Children's Books. "She was writing the book for herself." Instead, she's written one for millions. —*Troy Patterson/Photo illustration by Matt Mahurin*

JULIA
ROBERTS

In 1999, Julia Roberts had to do the impossible. She had to stand up, in front of paying audiences, look into Hugh Grant's eyes, and say "I'm just a girl…standing in front of a boy…asking him to love her." No. Julia Roberts is many things to many moviegoers, but *just a girl* is something she will never be. Julia Roberts, at 32, is a movie star from her gleaming surface to the marrow of her over-photographed cheekbones. *Just a girl* is not quite to be believed. Which, of course, is what made the line work. There isn't much that hasn't worked for Roberts lately. In 1990, the first time that EW chose her as an Entertainer of the Year, *Pretty Woman* had just heralded her arrival. Roberts, our writer said, "has joined…the minuscule elite of actresses who can command more than $1 million a picture." Let's look at the stats for '99. First of all, we can update that $1 million to $20 million, and trim that "minuscule elite" to a party of one. Roberts is now the highest-paid actress in the world, and by any measure the most popular; this summer, *Notting Hill* and *Runaway Bride* became her sixth and seventh films to top $100 million at the U.S. box office, a feat achieved by no other actress in history. For good measure, she guest-starred opposite boyfriend Benjamin Bratt on TV's *Law & Order*, and won an Emmy nomination. That role was a welcome stretch, and her next movie, the courtroom drama *Erin Brockovich*, should be another. But on screen, she blazes most enduringly as an icon of romantic longing, so it's fitting that she ended this decade by making what were, in effect, sequels to the two defining romantic comedies of the 1990s: *Pretty Woman* and *Four Weddings and a Funeral*. Perhaps, one day, Roberts will be known as the kind of actress who vanishes into a role. Right now, we don't want her to vanish. We want her to be a movie star. As for that *just a girl* line, don't forget the words that precede it: "The 'fame' thing," she says, "…it isn't really *real*, you know?" Another lie. But she does have a way of making us believe. —*Mark Harris*

There is a fascinating flowchart tucked into the liner notes of *The Best of Santana*. It's like one of those ancestral trees you'd find folded up in a family Bible: It lists the 16 lineups of Santana between 1966 and 1984, and it attempts to trace the whereabouts of every wayward musician who's ever slapped a conga or stroked a bass in Carlos Santana's eternal samba-soul caravan. This is not an easy task. Rod Harper, the drummer in Santana's first lineup? "Disappeared." Leon Patillo, singer and pianist from Santana No. 9? "Vanished." For decades, a lot of Americans assumed that such a Jimmy Hoffa-esque fate had befallen the band's own namesake. That's ridiculous; Carlos Santana, a guy whose guitar licks are as instantly recognizable as the sear of jalapeño on your tongue, has been packing arenas for years. Not until 1999, however, did pop radio remember the mystic in its midst. Santana concocted a lineup of musicians who did not qualify as "vanished"—Lauryn Hill, Dave Matthews, Wyclef Jean, matchbox 20's Rob Thomas—and cut an album called *Supernatural*. What happened next constitutes the most astonishing comeback since John Travolta slurped a milk shake in *Pulp Fiction*. *Supernatural* ascended to the top of the *Billboard* album chart, generating a No. 1 single ("Smooth") and selling 4 million copies. In Spanish, the word for "miracle" is *milagro*. Carlos sees it that way. You can toss out all the marketing blather you want—"cross-demographic appeal," "Latin boom"—but this 52-year-old veteran of the original, riot-free Woodstock considers *Supernatural* the product of nothing less than cosmic intervention. "It's not chance or luck," he says. "It's something more paranormal—like divine synchronicity. My intention was to spread a spiritual virus." Spiritual serenity has helped the Mexican-born ax divinity make the most of his blessings. "The first time I was very angry, confused," he recalls. "By the time we got to Woodstock, it seems like one minute I was in high school, the next I was playing with Janis Joplin. It happened too fast. But now there's so much clarity and purpose I'm able to actually *enjoy* everything." —*Jeff Gordinier*

CARLOS
SANTANA

The audience cheers as the stage darkens. A hush descends on the set, the only sound the thump of a heartbeat: *Boom, boom...boom, boom.* "Now, for one million dollars, here's your question: How did a Brit quiz show called *Who Wants to Be a Millionaire* kick-start a third-place network, spawn a slew of copycats, devastate the competition, and mesmerize nearly 21 million viewers per episode, making it the TV sensation of the season?" (A) The brainteasers. They ranged from annoyingly easy ("What is your power source if you use solar energy?") to ridiculously arcane ("Which English king did Shakespeare refer to as Bolingbroke?"), but either way, America debated, dissected, discussed—*obsessed* over *Millionaire*'s puzzlers. "Perhaps what we proved is that there is no canon of American trivia," says exec producer Michael Davies. (B) The contestants. For once, TV's most gripping drama didn't unfold on *ER*—it took place in *Millionaire*'s hot seat. The show wisely exploited a vast resource: the American public. "The fact that contestants didn't have 'TV personalities' is why people relate to them," says Davies. (C) It's interactive fun. Unlike the isolation-boothed appeal of '50s quiz shows like *The $64,000 Question*, *Millionaire* was a we're-all-in-it-together affair—from polling the audience to dialing up friends. "It's a drama people can identify with because they can be there themselves," says cocreator Paul Smith. (D) *Reege!* "I thought I'd reached my little mountain peak with the [morning] show," says Regis Philbin, 66. "Then along comes this." Watching him enjoy his sweet success was our treat: Kathie Lee-free, he handled his emcee role with bravado, humor, and hammy gravitas. So what's it gonna be? A? B? C? D? Doesn't matter. The country has locked in its final answer, leaving other nets to cower in fear. And with ABC bringing back *Millionaire three* times a week in January, the games have only just begun. —*Dan Snierson/Photograph by Andrew Brusso*

WHO WANTS
TO BE A
MILLIONAIRE

9

DENZEL
WASHINGTON

Denzel Washington has played a doctor, a lawyer, a submarine officer—any number of authoritative figures; nobody does commanding reserve better. But Washington excels as men in physical or spiritual bondage. All three of his Oscar-nominated roles —in 1987's *Cry Freedom*, 1989's *Glory* (a Best Supporting Actor victory), and 1992's *Malcolm X*—cast him as oppressed rebels, men whose bodies were restrained but whose minds remained free. That description also applies to Washington's pair of powerful performances this year, as quadriplegic forensics expert Lincoln Rhyme in *The Bone Collector* and unjustly incarcerated boxer Rubin Carter in *The Hurricane*. "Denzel has command of his instrument, which is his body," says *Collector* director Phillip Noyce. "And he can play it like a violin." To prepare for the role of the bedridden Rhyme, Washington met with dozens of paralyzed people, ranging from a construction worker to Christopher Reeve. ("We basically just talked about what movies he's going to direct," he recalls. "Which is how it oughta be.") But while research may grease the wheels, a virtuoso turn runs on divine spark. In the film, Washington hardly moves a muscle, and yet he manages to turn Rhyme into both action hero and sex symbol: The scene in which costar Angelina Jolie lovingly strokes one of Washington's fingers stands as one of the year's most quietly erotic screen moments. In striking contrast, Washington takes on an intensely physical part in *The Hurricane*, as the fighter made famous by Bob Dylan's ballad of the same name. Prior to production, Washington dropped 44 pounds, achieving a brutally lean and sculpted physique. "I figured it was the last chance for me to play an athlete other than a chess player," says the 45-year-old actor. Carter may have been a middleweight, but Washington's performance should make him a heavyweight come awards time. "When I got these two roles, I went, 'Man, there's a real good opportunity here,'" Washington says. "What a one-two punch for an actor to go from a quadriplegic to a boxer." In both cases, he scored a knockout. —*Bruce Fretts*

The Dixie Chicks have sold more than 8 million copies of their Grammy-winning '98 debut, *Wide Open Spaces*, but it was their August '99 follow-up, *Fly*, that really made industry insiders take full measure of these raucous soul sisters (lead singer Natalie Maines, 25, banjo player Emily Robison, 27, and fiddler Martie Seidel, 30). Defying the sophomore jinx, *Fly* wafted its way up to No. 1 on the pop charts—not a surprise in itself, given the trio's hard touring and impressive displays of virtuosity. The shock was how *good* the album is: Ignoring the usual Nashville recipe—bake a dozen pop-inflected tunes delivered by Nashville cookie-cutter songwriting pros and serve chilled with studio professionalism—the Chicks instead served up hot 'n' steamy biscuits like "Goodbye Earl," their ode to offing an abusive husband, and "Sin Wagon," a yowling testament to "mattress dancin'." *Fly* coheres as a statement of independence in a genre whose stars are typically rewarded for their conformity. And bringing the fiddle and banjo back into mainstream country, while continuing to get airplay on narrowly programmed, pop-minded country stations, makes the Dixie Chicks this year's neo-trad heroines—a status certified in September with three Country Music Awards. "They take chances," says Buddy Miller, whose song "Hole in My Head" the Chicks found entirely in keeping with their let's-go-crazy brand of country. "I wrote that song with Jim Lauderdale on the way to the recording studio," admits Miller. "And the fact that they dug a tossed-off, nutty song—well, not many Nashville acts are willing to stick their necks out like that." Sticking their Chick-en necks out seems to be the plan. "The only way to please the people is to please ourselves," says Maines. "After you sell as many records as we did with *Wide Open Spaces*, you can pretty much do what you want," adds Robison. "In fact, I don't understand why so many country acts, as they become more popular, take fewer chances—they don't want to mess with the style that got them famous. We look at each other and think, Hey, we're all *about* messing with styles." *—KT/Photograph by Jeffrey Thurnher*

THE DIXIE
CHICKS

MAINES   ROBISON   SEIDEL

SPIKE
JONZE

In a year dominated by teen pop, beefy wrestlers, and a sixtyish quizmaster called Reege, how did an iconoclastic music-video director named Spike Jonze manage to bust through the clutter? Let's review: First, there was his award-winning Fatboy Slim video, "Praise You." Then there was his big-screen acting turn in *Three Kings*. And, of course, there was Jonze's feature directorial debut, *Being John Malkovich*, an astonishingly original, critically cheered film about a mysterious portal that puts people inside actor John Malkovich's head (played, in an inspired bit of Method casting, by Malkovich himself). And he still found time to marry Sofia Coppola last summer. Yet for all the notice, Jonze has remained maddeningly mysterious. Aside from a few basic biographical factoids—born Adam Spiegel in 1969, heir to the Spiegel catalog fortune, former competitive skateboarder, helmer of groundbreaking Beastie Boys and Puff Daddy videos and commercials (notably a Nissan spot in which a dog pushes a man in a recliner)—very little is known about him. "He's like Andy Kaufman," says *Kings* costar Ice Cube. "You don't know when he's in or when he's out [of character]." Like Kaufman's Tony Clifton, Jonze has an alter ego—a spastic dance-troupe leader named Richard Koufay. Also like Kaufman, Jonze takes his not-so-secret second identity very seriously. According to Fatboy Slim (a.k.a. Norman Cook), calling Jonze and Koufay the same person is "libelous." Don't bother asking Jonze to explain it. "I don't know what you're talking about," he says sheepishly when asked if he and Koufay are one and the same. He isn't any more forthcoming about his artistic process: "I think about what the idea is and whatever the best way to execute the idea is." *Now* we get it. Fortunately, the work speaks for itself. Any other director might use his new cachet to jump into a big-budget blockbuster. But Jonze is showing no signs of going by the book. Next, he's producing *Human Nature*, a drama about a woman who becomes entirely covered with hair. He may also be returning to his MTV roots for a rumored new series on the music channel. Details of the show are still (what else?) secret, but its tentative title sure sounds like another clutter buster: *Jack Ass*. —Tricia Johnson

Wes Bentley's *American Beauty* costar Kevin Spacey bolted Juilliard's drama school after three years. But it only took Bentley one year before he felt he'd gotten everything the august institution had to offer. "I have friends who are still there," he says, "and that's fine. I had to get off the bus." Ever since, the strikingly blue-eyed 21-year-old has been riding steadily to stardom. After a bit part in *Beloved*, he landed a lead role as a killer in *The White River Kid*, an as-yet-unreleased drama starring Antonio Banderas. But it was as *Beauty*'s handsome, preternaturally self-possessed teen dope dealer that Bentley radiated star quality. Coming up is *Soul Survivors*, a *Sixth Sense*-ish thriller about a college kid involved in a car crash. Bentley hasn't mapped his journey beyond that, but he plans to bypass action flicks. "I think filmmakers emphasize visuals to the point they forget characters," he says. "We need a resurgence of the actor." *—Steve Daly/Photograph by Lance Staedler*

WES
BENTLEY

CHRISTOPHER
MELONI

For Christopher Meloni, 1999 was the year he proved he could do more than just be good at being bad. Viewers who watched the D.C. native strut his dangerously dreamy stuff as Jimmy Liery, an irresistible creep from Kim Delaney's past on *NYPD Blue*, or as Chris Keller, the underhanded inmate on *Oz*, had no idea he could play nice. But Meloni, 38, settled seamlessly into *Runaway Bride* as Julia Roberts' charming-but-blockheaded fiancé—until she sidelined him for Richard Gere (pretty dopey woman?). And this fall, Meloni landed on the right side of the justice system in NBC's *Law & Order: Special Victims Unit* as Det. Elliot Stabler, a married-with-kids sex-crimes investigator. "He's a rock-solid guy, with a great capacity for compassion, the ironic, and the absurd," the actor has said of Stabler. Sounds like Meloni himself, who, by the way, hasn't reformed all his bad-boy tendencies: Look for him as Keller in *Oz*'s upcoming fourth season. *—Joe Dziemianowicz/Photograph by Alison Dyer*

HALEY JOEL
OSMENT

A suggestion for M. Night Shyamalan, the writer-director behind the $270 million-plus sensation *The Sixth Sense*: If the filmmaking thing doesn't work out, try the talent-scout biz. Moviegoers have Shyamalan to thank for casting Haley Joel Osment, the 11-year-old wunderkind whose performance as Cole Sear, a kid scared stiff by his ability to see ghosts, has forever raised the bar for prepubescent thespians (his was the mouth that voiced the year's most shivery line: "I see dead people"). In *Sense*, Osment gave much more than the typical trained-pet child performance. In successfully suffering the supernatural heebie-jeebies, the young actor articulated with remarkable nuance the darker arc of childhood: Just listen to the heartbreak in such lines as "I just don't want to be afraid anymore." This kid can act—though Shyamalan dares to go one step further: "We've had child prodigies in music and science. Now we finally have one in acting." Next up, Osment will costar opposite Kevin Spacey in the upcoming *Pay It Forward*. Until then, guess he'll continue to negotiate the sixth grade. —*Jeff Jensen/Photograph by Mojgan B. Azimi*

JULIA
STILES

Consider every up-and-coming actress between 16 and 21. Now eliminate those who've played virginity-losing, bikini-sporting, dagger-avoiding ingenues. Who's left? That would be Julia Stiles, 18, an actress who happily swapped slashers for Shakespeare in 1999 and made herself *the* one to watch. As an endearingly tough teenager in *10 Things I Hate About You* (a modern go at the Bard's *The Taming of the Shrew*), Stiles proved her comedic range, and her heartrending depiction of a teenage mother in the miniseries *The '60s* helped earn NBC a ratings love-in. Now, after two more Shakespeare adaptations—next year's *O* (a high school-set *Othello*) and *Hamlet*, starring Ethan Hawke—the onetime Tide commercial actress has opted to star opposite Freddie Prinze Jr. in the romantic comedy *Down to You*. "I don't rely on anything," says Stiles, who almost gave up showbiz when she lost the role of Claudia in 1994's *Interview With the Vampire* (it went to Kirsten Dunst). "It's such a temperamental business; you can make it one minute and not make it the next." So just in case, she's got a backup plan. "I'm into politics," she says. "If you think about it, politicians are certainly another form of actors." Classically put. —*Jessica Shaw*

She walked on walls. She dressed in shrink-wrapped thermoplastic. She kicked butt. Most crucially of all, Carrie-Anne Moss, in her career-making turn as Trinity in *The Matrix*, did it all with a sensuous insouciance that coolly glazed the film's fierce digital pyrotechnics and sexed-up sci-fi considerably—maybe irrevocably. Like one of her mind-blowing escapes in the movie, Moss' leap into stardom is sizable, not to mention startling. "I was ready to do TV and the occasional bad movie for the rest of my life," says the 32-year-old former denizen of Fox's unfortunate *Models Inc.* "And then this happened." This, indeed: *The Matrix* has grossed nearly $400 million worldwide. As a result, the actress has become the ultimate futuristic harpy, a sort of next-generation Linda Hamilton, pairing up with Val Kilmer for another sci-fi thriller, *Red Planet* (due later this year), and, of course, there are the next two *Matrix* installments. "I'd like to do [a project] that doesn't involve me wearing PVC," notes Moss of her typical vinyl-style costumes. "But I suppose that can wait." —*Will Lee*

CARRIE-ANNE
MOSS

JIMMY KIMMEL AND ADAM CAROLLA
'THE MAN SHOW'

How to explain the caveman-like footprints left on the landscape this year by Comedy Central's boorishly amusing variety series *The Man Show*? Why, it's simple physics: For every action, there is an equal and opposite reaction. In this age of uplifting She TV (*Touched by an Angel*, *Any Day Now*), there had to be a truckload of disgruntled men just dying to tap a keg and revel in their own glorious guy-ness. Enter overgrown frat boys Jimmy Kimmel and Adam Carolla—a Beavis to the other's Butt-head, a Bill to the other's Ted—who entertained and offended with farting monkeys, chicks bouncing on trampolines, and crafty "man-o-vations" (like golf tees made out of beef jerky, and Pamela Anderson Lee masks for dogs that wander into the room while you're, you know… getting in touch with yourself). "It's comedy meets titillation," snickers Carolla, who is also known to cable viewers as the cohost of MTV's *Loveline*. Adds his buddy Kimmel (a.k.a. the sidekick on Comedy Central's *Win Ben Stein's Money*), "If anyone's threatened by the show, they're nuts. It's just a half-hour comedy show on a cable network. It's not gonna take away their right to vote." In that case, party on, dudes. —*Dan Snierson/Photograph by Gail Albert Halaban*

MELINA
KANAKAREDES

She'd already locked lips with *NYPD Blue*'s Jimmy Smits and lathered up on *Guiding Light*. But it wasn't until she donned Dr. Sydney Hansen's stethoscope on NBC's unexpected mid-season hit *Providence* that Melina Kanakaredes became more than "that actress with the luscious locks and the hard-to-say name." With her inviting, best-girlfriend appeal, Kanakaredes, 32, rose above the drama's critical lashing (one wag labeled it "must-flee TV") and helped *Providence* nab NBC's highest ratings for any new drama since *ER*. "Look up *adorable*—no, make that *genuine*—in the dictionary, and you'll find Melina's picture there," says *Providence* costar Tom Verica. "You can't help but gravitate to her." Robert De Niro proved no exception: The actor hand-picked Kanakaredes for the female lead in his upcoming film, *15 Minutes*, due in the fall. "As far as [great] years go, this one's right up there," says Kanakaredes. "But you know how crazy things are in this business. I could be back to waitressing next week." Prognosis: unlikely. —*Shawna Malcom/Photograph by Jilly Wendell*

THE CAST OF
'AMERICAN PIE'

Blame *There's Something About Mary*. That megahit paved the way for the out-there raunch that made *American Pie* a phenomenon—an $11 million high school sex romp that's earned $101 million. "It seems people have taken to us because we're this quirky little smut movie," *Pie* producer Chris Weitz joked to EW (brother Paul was billed as director). Maybe so. But while *Pie* made a crusty genre fresh again (The plot: Four guys vow to lose their virginity by prom night), it also sparked the careers of its apple-cheeked stars, from left, Thomas Ian Nicholas, Alyson Han-

nigan, Jason Biggs, Mena Suvari, and Chris Klein. "People ask, 'Has your life changed?' I'm like, uh, yeah!" says Klein, who also starred in *Election*. That's really the case for Suvari, who earned raves as Kevin Spacey's fantasy girl in *American Beauty* and who reteams with Biggs next year in *Loser*. Nicholas and Hannigan (*Buffy the Vampire Slayer*) do the indie thing next in *Cutaway* and *Beyond the City Limits*, respectively, as Klein joins Leelee Sobieski in the romance *Here on Earth*. Klein sums it up: "It was a blessing for all of us." —*Tricia Johnson/Photograph by Christy Bush*

MELISSA
BANK

There are best-selling page-turners, the novels you trudge through because they're "good for you." And then there are soul bibles, the books that compel you to buy a copy for every friend you have. Such was Melissa Bank's debut, *The Girls' Guide to Hunting and Fishing*, seven short stories about one romantically challenged woman. In Jane Rosenal, Bank, 39, has created a heroine for our time, a chick with the wry humor of Bridget Jones, the poignancy of Ally McBeal, and the bawdy bite of *Sex and the City*. "It was kind of scary," Bank says of her 15-week run on the *New York Times* best-seller list and her movie deal with Francis Ford Coppola. "You write for a long time in your dark room, and all of a sudden there's a bright light on you." We think that's called the limelight. —*Jessica Shaw*

CHRISTINA
AGUILERA

Naysaying adults dismiss teen pop as Mickey Mouse stuff, and the success of Christina Aguilera, 19, isn't likely to change their minds: Like her chief rival, Britney Spears, Aguilera rose to international pop stardom after a stint on the Disney Channel's *Mickey Mouse Club*. But don't judge her by her catchy-if-lightweight single, "Genie in a Bottle," or mistake her for the latest blond flavor of the month. This ambitious Pennsylvanian is in it for the long haul, and she's got the chops to go the distance. Aguilera has already drawn comparisons to a young Mariah Carey on the strength of a debut album, titled simply *Christina Aguilera*, which is deeper than you suspect. Ballads like "So Emotional" reveal a depth and maturity that indicate she may be around long after other bubblegum acts have been chewed up and spit out. And she's got both eyes on the future. "I always want to shock people throughout my career," Aguilera has said. "Like Madonna." Remember—they said the Material Girl wouldn't last, either. —*Tom Sinclair/Photograph by Alison Dyer*

GREAT
PERFORMANCES

THE CAST OF
'SEX AND THE CITY'

My goodness, the mouths on these girls! The four fearless women of HBO's comedy *Sex and the City* (from left, Kim Cattrall, Kristin Davis, Sarah Jessica Parker, and Cynthia Nixon) chatted with hilarious frankness this year about everything under the Kama Sutra: oral sex, penis size, pubic-hair topiary, you name it. Sure, the critically adored show—created by Darren Star about single, sexually adventurous Manhattan power gals—also featured impressive acting, the chicest of fashions, glitzy New York locales, and cleverly nuanced plots about friendship and loyalty. But did we mention the funny sex talk? It got so graphic, even the stars couldn't escape embarrassment. During the show's rehearsals, the demure Parker would whisper the script's dirtiest words—much to the amusement of costar Chris Noth. "Chris is like, 'C'mon, Sarah, you can say it!'" laughs Parker. Or consider Davis, who wouldn't let her family see the series' naughtiest bits. "My mom has to call me, and I have to approve of the episode or not approve." As for us, we approve of it all. —*A. J. Jacobs/Photograph by Guy Aroch*

JOAN
CUSACK

"Maybe it's having a family and getting older." That's how Joan Cusack, 37, explains her decision to veer her famously quirky career (*Addams Family Values*, *In & Out*) onto a serious track this year. She got in touch with her dark side as Tim Robbins' creepily devoted wife in the thriller *Arlington Road*, played Julia Roberts' levelheaded sidekick "who would say things a real best friend would say" in *Runaway Bride*, and gave a sober turn as a government clerk in the Depression-era drama *Cradle Will Rock* (directed by Robbins), in which she held her own amid a power ensemble that included Susan Sarandon, John Turturro, and her brother, John. Not bad for someone who made her first impression as the "back-brace girl" in 1984's *Sixteen Candles*. "I'm not just a wacky, goofy girl in life, so it's nice to have some depth to what I do," says Cusack, who's expecting a second child in May (her son Dylan John is now 2). Looks like the cradle has rocked the actress into contentment. —*Tricia Johnson*

MOLLY
SHANNON

"A firecracker." That's how director Bruce McCulloch describes Molly Shannon. No kidding: The combustible comedian—who's been a *Saturday Night Live* cast member for six seasons—exploded onto the big screen in 1999 with three attention-getting gigs: *Analyze This*, as a neurotic ex-girlfriend; *Never Been Kissed*, in which she played Drew Barrymore's sexy, savvy bud; and, of course, *Superstar*, where she led the goings-on as Mary Katherine Gallagher, the parochial school pariah responsible for the actress' breakout success on *SNL*. A funny girl with an unfunny past (her mom, sister, and cousin were killed in a car accident three decades ago), the Ohio-bred Shannon, 34, has dubbed her signature schoolgirl "a product of my childhood: anxious, exaggerated—a more anxious, exaggerated version of myself. I don't think she thinks of herself as a loser. She just perseveres." Ditto Shannon, who ends this year by filming the anticipated *Dr. Seuss' How the Grinch Stole Christmas*, in which she plays one of Whoville's finest—and no doubt funniest. Ka-*boom*! —*Joe Dziemianowicz/Photograph by Stephanie Rausser*

Is it possible to discuss Jon Stewart without mentioning self-deprecation? Probably not. The New Jersey native, who cut his teeth as a stand-up comic, has dissed himself about being a lousy actor, overly hairy, and, most often, short. Do we buy his I'm-not-worthy antics? Not really. This multitalented multitasker rates props for his wacky humor book *Naked Pictures of Famous People* and movies like the surprisingly sweet *Playing by Heart* and the comic megahit *Big Daddy*. Most impressive, though, are the smarts and charm he's exuded all year as the new host (replacing Craig Kilborn) of Comedy Central's TV-news lampoon *The Daily Show*. "It gives me the opportunity to not have to sit up at 2 a.m. in bed and try to find a place to get the joke out of my head," Stewart, 37, has said of his gig. Bet his four-day week, tons of time off for other projects, and a $1.5 million annual salary—huge for a cable guy—don't hurt either. Jon Stewart may still be only 5 foot 7, but he's finally livin' large. —*Joe Dziemianowicz*

JON
STEWART

THE BACKSTREET
BOYS

If nothing else, these five big boppers, with an average age of 23, have proven that they're an intrepid bunch. While everyone else in Hollywood was steering clear of *The Phantom Menace*—presumed to be the summer's entertainment juggernaut—the Backstreet Boys took the galactic prequel head-on, releasing their second U.S. record, *Millennium*, the same week the George Lucas opus opened. And clearly kids had saved their allowance for the occasion: *Millennium* sold a record-breaking 1.13 million copies in its debut week. Fueled by the impossibly catchy (and impossibly incomprehensible) single "I Want It That Way," the disc went on to be certified platinum seven times, ranking it as one of the best-selling CDs of the year and securing the Boys' position as the new voice of pop. Their fans snatched up BSB concert tickets at a similarly frenzied rate: On Aug. 14 their entire tour sold out almost within an hour (the grand total: 765,000 tickets). Now who do you think the Force was with? —*Dave Karger/Photograph by Andrew Southam*

MARGARET

CHO

No performer in '99 demonstrated the healing power of honesty more than Margaret Cho. In her captivating Off Broadway one-woman show, *I'm the One That I Want*, the Korean-American comedian chronicles weight and drinking battles, man trouble, and a near-fatal stint on her failed '95 sitcom *All-American Girl*. Savage and *seriously* funny, Cho emerges as an Aesop of edgy neurosis, turning stand-up into an anthem for survival. —*Jess Cagle/Photographs by Sean Murphy*

JANET

McTEER

Actresses love full-bodied mother roles with scenes of high dudgeon, high spirits, and high catharsis, but few have played them with such unactressy abandon as Janet McTeer in *Tumbleweeds*. As a restless single mom going from one unsuccessful romance to another, the British stage star, entirely believable as a Southern gal, demonstrates that rarest of qualities among big mamas: a lack of pretension. Awards ought to tumble her way. —*Lisa Schwarzbaum/Photograph by Barron Claiborne*

CHER

Used to be, you could always count on two things in life: death and taxes. Now, make it three: death, taxes, and...Cher. This year, after her smash album *Believe*, a smash hit single of the same name, a sold-out summer tour, headlining VH1's *Divas Live '99*, and her first movie in three years, *Tea With Mussolini*, Cher solidified her rep as queen of the comeback. At 53, she's admittedly seen more ups, downs, and ups again than just about anyone else around— from TV megastar to infomercial hostess, kitschy Vegas headliner to Oscar-winning actress. "That's my life," Cher told EW. "That's always been my life. Sometimes it's a hassle, sometimes it's fun. You can't predict stuff." Except, of course, that she will survive. —*Betty Cortina*

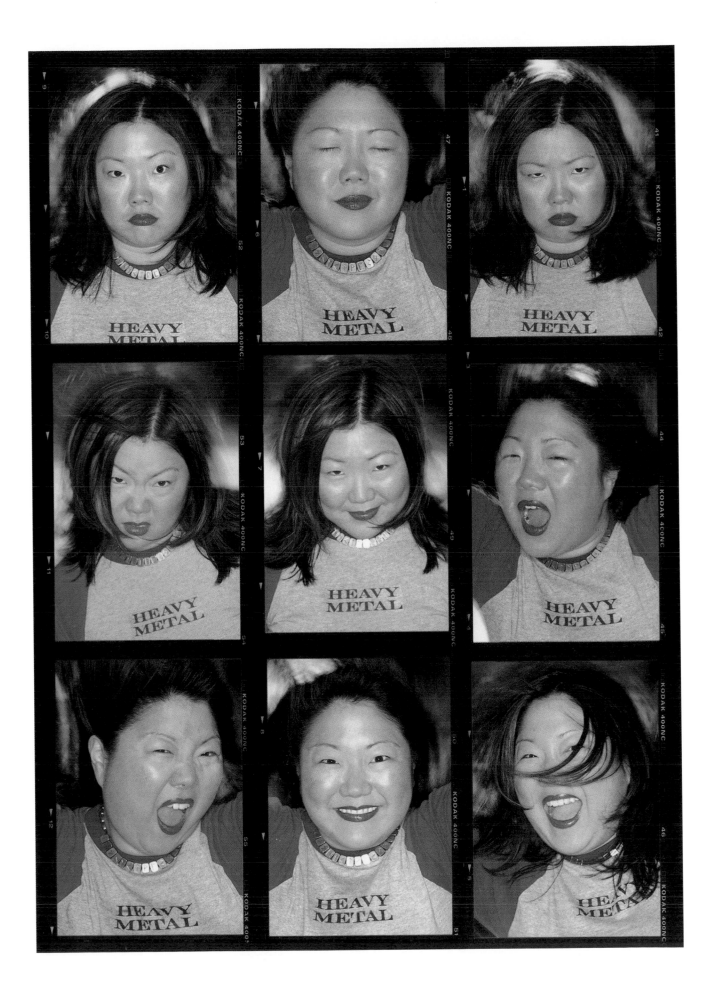

RUSSELL
CROWE

Suppose you took a chance and informed against a monstrous evil…and that evil struck back. Your life is shoved through a meat grinder while your supposed protector cowers on the sidelines. As *The Insider*'s real-life tobacco whistle-blower Jeffrey Wigand, Crowe conjures a performance brimming with flint and terror. And like fellow alchemist Robert De Niro, he makes it look confoundingly easy. —*Daniel Fierman/Photograph by Yariv Milchan/CPI*

JEREMY
NORTHAM

Cheeky Rupert Everett was supposed to steal the show. At the very least, the lustrous Cate Blanchett was meant to steal the scenes. But in the end, it was Northam—all liquid eyes, slow-burn charisma, and touching fallibility—who made off with our hearts as Robert Chilton, Oscar Wilde's *Ideal Husband*. The Brit donned a waistcoat yet again for David Mamet's *The Winslow Boy*, this time sexing up a pompous lawyer. Who knew rectitude could be such a turn-on? —*Tricia Johnson*

RENE
RUSSO

It wasn't just her heat, it was her humidity. This summer, playing well-heeled insurance investigator Catherine Banning opposite Pierce Brosnan in a remake of *The Thomas Crown Affair*, Rene Russo turned in the season's definitive sultry performance, elevating herself from ex-model to topflight actress. Russo, 45, who'd previously appeared as glorified eye candy in films like *Lethal Weapon 3* and *Tin Cup*, had a little trouble accessing her inner femme fatale. "I don't normally lead with my sexuality," she says of the role. "I'm actually a nervous wreck." Director John McTiernan had to challenge Russo into the part, accusing her of "neutering" herself in earlier work. McTiernan, who envisioned a Lauren Bacall-style performance, made Russo redo a take when she merely diverted her eyes. He even went so far as to recommend some unconventional inspiration: "He actually had me go see a madam," she confesses. And, most courageously, she had to bare her soul—and her skin—in a heavy selection of nude scenes. "That wasn't so tough," recalls Russo. "At first, you walk around with a towel hiding everything. Half a day into it, I said, 'Oh, f--- it. I'll pretend I'm at a nudist camp.'"—*Andrew Essex*

HILARY
SWANK

And we thought only lightweights came from that neighborhood. Until this year, Hilary Swank, 25, was best known for playing single mom Carly on *Beverly Hills, 90210.* Then came her lauded turn in the unsettling true-life drama *Boys Don't Cry,* and suddenly the actress had earned residence among Hollywood's heavy hitters. As Brandon Teena, a young girl who lived as a young man in rural Nebraska until she was exposed and murdered, Swank was a revelation: Her physical transformation was utterly convincing, her performance heartbreaking. "I've been waiting for a role where I could do something totally different from myself," says Swank, who prepared for the part by cutting her hair, borrowing her husband's clothes (she's married to Rob Lowe's brother, actor Chad Lowe), and assuming a male alter ego for 30 days in Los Angeles, where she lives. "Brandon is really inspiring, because she lived her life fully in every single moment and followed a dream," adds the actress. "And that's what I want to be doing. When you're living your dream, you're exuding joy." —*Dave Karger/Photograph by Matthew Welch*

MARK
WAHLBERG

Before slipping into the snug slacks of Dirk Diggler, Mark Wahlberg seemed like a cursed cross between Rico Suave and Rodney Dangerfield—a former bubblegum rapper who couldn't get any respect. Now, two years after *Boogie Nights* showed the promise of a devastating actor trapped inside a Calvin Klein model's body, Wahlberg's raw and vulnerable performance in *Three Kings* has clinched his hard-won battle for approval. "I think things are finally a little different for me," Wahlberg says, then adds with a sly grin, "but I still don't mind proving people wrong." Problem is, after *Kings,* there aren't any naysayers left to convince. Pulled like a human wishbone between his greed and his morality, Wahlberg's Sgt. Troy Barlow is the film's most unpredictably high-voltage character—he's as much a live wire as the electric device the Iraqis use to torture him. But perhaps the biggest props come from George Clooney, who's reteaming with his *Kings* costar both in *The Perfect Storm* and as a producer of Wahlberg's rock satire *Metal God.* Notes Clooney, "If you're gonna hitch your career to somebody, I don't mind doing it to Mark." —*Chris Nashawaty/Photograph by Norman Jean Roy*

THE BIG-SCREEN DEBUT OF
'SOUTH PARK'

Who knew Satan was a song-and-dance man? Or that Saddam Hussein had a soft side? Or that Winona Ryder could commit unspeakable acts with Ping-Pong balls? You may think something is seriously wrong with *South Park* creators Matt Stone and Trey Parker, but we defy you to watch their 1999 movie, *South Park: Bigger, Longer & Uncut*, which grossed a surprising $52 million, without being at least slightly amused. And even if you're completely insulted by their animated depiction of the "quiet little white-bread redneck mountain town" of South Park, Colo., you've at least got to give Parker and Stone points for bravery: Nobody, no matter how powerful or famous, is safe from a good *South Park* jab. Not Bill Gates, not the MPAA ratings board (which wanted to label the film NC-17), not even the Baldwin family. Are the filmmakers worried about repercussions? Nah. Says Stone, "If we get booed and kicked out of this town tomorrow, we can leave with our heads held up high, because we did everything the way we wanted to do it." —*David Hochman*

EUGENE
LEVY

What's a dad to do when his son abuses baked goods? As the bumbling father who doesn't always know best, *American Pie*'s Eugene Levy helped turn Paul and Chris Weitz's $102 million summer fling into a distinctly family affair. Levy, the bushy-browed *SCTV* alum (the Canadian comedy troupe's graduates include Martin Short, John Candy, and Rick Moranis), has played the fool in a variety of goofy classics from *Splash* to *Waiting for Guffman*. As a comic vet, he was a tad nervous about portraying a patiently loving pop in a movie written by a couple of neophyte filmmakers. "The script read a little, um, out there," Levy, 53, recalls. By the time the cast came together for rehearsals, the actor had changed his mind. "I wound up trusting [the Weitz brothers'] comedic taste implicitly." The secret to his fatherly humor? A little old-fashioned love. "He really meant well," Levy says of his character. "Any dad would be concerned about what that kid was doing to his dessert." —*Andrew Essex*

HALLIE
EISENBERG

Not many actresses can say they've worked opposite such leading men as Robin Williams and Al Pacino. Even fewer can say they've done so before their eighth birthday. Except Hallie Eisenberg, that is, whose one-in-a-million precociousness and refreshingly unself-conscious screen presence landed the 7-year-old choice roles in this year's *Bicentennial Man* with Williams ("He taught me how to improvise," notes the actress) and *The Insider* starring Pacino ("Sometimes he looks scary, but he's really nice," she confirms). Then again, Eisenberg's biggest career boost may have come from her priceless crop of TV spots for Pepsi, featuring the spokescutie (previously seen in spots for cable's Independent Film Channel) as a savvy soda customer who assumes the voices of Marlon Brando, Isaac Hayes, and, in her favorite spot, Aretha Franklin. "I love to dance," explains Eisenberg, who says she didn't need vats of the caffeinated stuff to plow through umpteen takes of hoofing it to the "Joy of Cola" tune. Instead, she says she has "natural energy." We'll drink to that. —*Dave Karger*

If you were partaking of the steady diet of news-channel retrospectives, it often seemed that 1999 was just an appetizer for that big banquet known as The Millennium. But, in fact, as the year counted down to that ultimate tick of the clock, it had some truly momentous occasions all its own. Some were revelatory (Monica Lewinsky coming clean to Barbara Walters during a *20/20* interview); others were almost beyond comprehension (the nation coming to grips with the killings at Columbine High School, the world grieving the loss of America's first son, John F. Kennedy Jr.). And then there were the events that turned the entertainment world into the kind of feast that could satisfy so many different tastes. Bruce

THE
YEAR
IN
REVIEW

Springsteen and the E Street Band revived rock—or, at least, the rock concert-as-event—and everyone sang the praises of HBO's Mob drama *The Sopranos*. The Force grew even stronger thanks to *The Phantom Menace*, and a quiet movie about a little boy's ghostly visions became a box office force to be reckoned with. Meanwhile, a sexual psychodrama starring gorgeous marrieds Tom Cruise and Nicole Kidman turned audiences...off, of all things. And who would have guessed that the supreme Master of His Domain, Jerry Seinfeld, would finally succumb to—*gasp!*—the M-word? (Not that there's anything wrong with that.) For your 1999 flashback pleasure, turn the page to discover more of the year that was. *Bon appétit.*

Debbie Matenopoulos
DISAPPEARS FROM 'THE VIEW'

At first it was, like, okay. When ditsy twenty-something Debbie Matenopoulos vacated her cohosting gig on Barbara Walters' morning gabfest *The View*, the move was portrayed as a mutual decision. Matenopoulos gushed: "I owe everything to Barbara for being like a mother." Walters clucked back: "She's an adorable girl." For sure, but perhaps that's not exactly what Walters, the show's executive producer, was thinking on days when the "adorable girl" offered some of her famously astute observations. Like when guest Lucy Lawless, star of *Xena: Warrior Princess*, performed her trademark screech and Matenopoulos remarked: "No wonder all the lesbians like you." Soon Matenopoulos' sudden departure gained watercooler steam: The benevolent argued that a show offering a sampling of American womanhood should have allowed for the stupid girl, and *Saturday Night Live*

BLOND SIDED Matenopoulos with Joy Behar

was provided with an endless string of *View* parodies. The best: Cameron Diaz, as Matenopoulos, tries to find her way out of a canvas bag—and fails. After a near five-month-long and well-publicized search, Matenopoulos was replaced in May with Lisa Ling, 26, a former TV news reporter who won the job over seven other on-air applicants. Too bad: Those *SNL* skits were good viewing.

George Clooney
SAYS GOODBYE TO 'ER'

Just like his dreamy chin-down, eyes-up stare, George Clooney's decision to hang up his scrubs after five seasons on *ER* caused more than a few coronary flutters. Not to mention props from the Nielsens. The departure of County General's resident bad boy was spread out over three February sweeps episodes that earned NBC some of its highest ratings of the season for the must-see medical drama. And the final installment—in which Dr. Ross pleads with girlfriend Nurse Hathaway (Julianna Margulies) to leave with him—finally allowed the commitment-shy hunk to show signs of a romantic cure. Then again, it was precisely his your-mother-warned-you-about-me air that fans loved. How else to delight in those moments when he redeemed himself? "I could do five scenes of nothing but stupid, despicable things," Clooney told EW. "Then I'd turn around and say, 'You leave that kid alone!' and everybody would go 'Yeah!'" Whether viewers—okay, *women*—will give such heart-stopping devotion to Croatian actor Goran Visnjic, *ER*'s new Dr. Dreamboat, remains to be seen. But at least we'll have something to drool over while we find out.

01.12.99
MAIDEN VOYAGE
Britney Spears' album *...Baby One More Time* is released and soon tops *Billboard*'s album chart, aided by its titular single. The teen queen becomes the first debut artist to conquer both the No.1 album and singles spots simultaneously.

01.12.99
FRUMP ROAST
Linda Tripp tops Mr. Blackwell's worst-dressed list, proving conclusively that wearing a wire doesn't make you fashionable.

01.15.99
ODB POLICE BLOTTER (No. 1)
Wu-Tang Clan rapper Ol' Dirty Bastard (a.k.a. Big Baby Jesus, a.k.a. Russell Jones) is charged with attempted murder after a police shoot-out in Brooklyn. ODB claims he wasn't even armed, and the charge is later dropped. Stay tuned.

01.19.99
AS THE WORM TURNS...
Dennis Rodman announces his retirement from basketball.

01.20.99
...AND TURNS
Rodman says he's changed his mind about retiring.

01.24.99
JOLTIN' JOE
HAS LEFT, AND—WHOOPS!
During an episode of *Dateline*, NBC mistakenly reports Joe DiMaggio's death in a crawl across the bottom of the screen. About 15 minutes later, another crawl apologizes for the error.

01.26.99
GOING SOUTH
Pamela Anderson Lee says she's ending her South American tour after being mobbed by nearly 2,500 Uruguayan boys. In the U.S., Lee gets medical attention for injuries sustained when a rock was thrown at her head.

01.27.99
LIVER LET DIE
In a rare untelevised event, legendary stuntman Evel Knievel daringly exchanges his old liver, ravaged by hepatitis C, for a new healthy one.

01.28.99
BRIDE OF CHUCKIE?
Prince Charles and Camilla Parker Bowles make their first official public appearance as a couple, outside the Ritz Hotel in London.

BUCKLE UP

01.31.99
"OUCH" PREVENTION
E.T., the J.D. Salinger of extraterrestrials, makes his much-anticipated return to pop culture in a Progressive Insurance "Buckle Up America" ad campaign, which debuts during the Super Bowl.

01.31.99
A BOWL OF CHER
Riding high on her hit single "Believe," Cher kicks off Super Bowl XXXIII with a husky rendition of the national anthem. Gloria Estefan and Stevie Wonder perform at halftime, and, as an afterthought, the Denver Broncos tromp the Atlanta Falcons 34–19.

GOLD COAST Benigni hands it to America; below, Ford bestows Best Picture honors; Best Director Spielberg's V for Victory couldn't save *Private Ryan* from defeat. Opposite page: Lynn Redgrave celebrates with *Gods and Monsters* maker Bill Condon (left); Davis blooms into a pregame hostess.

THE 71st ANNUAL
Academy Awards

It was an Oscar race that was, well, a genuine race—a showdown between the WWII epic *Saving Private Ryan* and the charming period comedy *Shakespeare in Love*. And when the final moment arrived during March 21's 71st Annual Academy Awards ceremony, no one looked more surprised than Best Picture presenter Harrison Ford as he dangled the last envelope. Just a few moments earlier, Steven Spielberg had accepted the Best Director Oscar for *Ryan* (an honor he also received for 1994's Best Picture, *Schindler's List*), and suddenly 45.6 million viewers were sure the film would take home top honors too. But with a look of puzzlement, Ford delivered the unexpected news: The Oscar would go to...*Shakespeare in Love*. The victory ended a marketing-campaign duel between *Love*'s Miramax and *Ryan*'s DreamWorks (the former's guerrilla-warfare tactics were rumored to be significantly more expensive, but studio

cochairman Harvey Weinstein just scoffed, "I think you should get in trouble in this town for *not* supporting your films") and sparked endless industry and fan debate. (Was Spielberg robbed?) At DreamWorks' Oscar party at Barnaby's, a flack threw a black shawl over the TV after *Shakespeare* won; over at the Polo Lounge, the triumphant Miramax folks danced until dawn. Not that the evening was without many other great moments: There was Geena Davis' debut as a pregame hostess; a too-teary Gwyneth Paltrow accepting her Best Actress award and the dignified Judi Dench receiving her Supporting Actress statuette; an ecstatic Roberto Benigni vaulting across chairs; and, of course, hostess Whoopi Goldberg, who spent the night changing into an assortment of outlandish costumes from various nominated films. It certainly made us wonder: What's Billy Crystal doing next year?

02.04.99
SHAM AND DIANE
Diane Sawyer apologizes for secretly recording her coworkers' polite but mendacious responses to her deliberately awful "homemade" chili. The tape is for a *20/20* segment on lying, but ABC kills it after the staff expresses concern.

02.10.99
DON'T ASK, DON'T TELETUBBY
"Role-modeling the gay lifestyle is damaging to the moral lives of children," says clergyman and concerned TV viewer Jerry Falwell, after a column in his newsletter warns that Tinky Winky, the purple, purse-toting Teletubby, is a "gay role model."

02.11.99
ANOTHER MONICA SCANDAL
Secret's out! The furtive dalliance between Chandler and Monica is finally revealed to all of their pals on *Friends*.

02.15.99
THE SWEET 'LIFE'
On its way to Oscar gold, *Life Is Beautiful* becomes the highest-grossing foreign-language film ever released in North America, taking in more than $24 million and surpassing former champ *Il Postino*. Roberto Benigni's Holocaust fable will eventually nab over $229 million worldwide.

02.18.99
ODB POLICE BLOTTER (No. 2)
He's Ol'. He's Dirty. And he's under arrest. Again. The Wu-Tang Clansman is jailed for wearing a bulletproof vest (illegal attire for felons in California) and released the same day on bail.

02.19.99
SPAWN OF SPICE
Spice Girl Melanie Brown (a.k.a. Scary) gives birth to daughter Phoenix Chi in London.

David Blaine
GOES UNDERGROUND

Somewhere, Harry Houdini is jealous. When illusionist David Blaine buried himself alive for seven days in a sidewalk on Manhattan's Upper West Side, he became the kind of spectacle the famous escape artist would have loved. Deep within a two-ton, see-through, Plexiglas coffin, Blaine ate nothing, drank four tablespoons of water a day, breathed through a tube, and lived to tell the tale. Yet that wasn't the spellbinder's most astonishing trick. More astounding was how he hypnotized hardened New Yorkers (85,000 people visited, including Rosie O'Donnell, Regis Philbin, Edward Norton, and the *Today* show), levitated himself to stardom, and helped make magic—banished into geekdom—hip again. Blaine insisted his sojourn was a test of will, not a publicity stunt. (Houdini, his hero, had planned a similar feat but died before he could perform it.) Either way, the hype came in handy: Two days after his resurrection, the ABC special *David Blaine: Magic Man* drew an impressive 12.9 million viewers. Now Blaine's hoping to wave his wand and turn that success into a movie career. He's working on an autobiographical film, *Trick Monkey*, which he's described as "the *Rocky* of magic. It's about a young magician fighting his way up." Looks like Blaine won't be performing a vanishing act any time soon.

NEW YORK UNDERCOVER Blaine bids adieu to spacious living as he prepares for burial

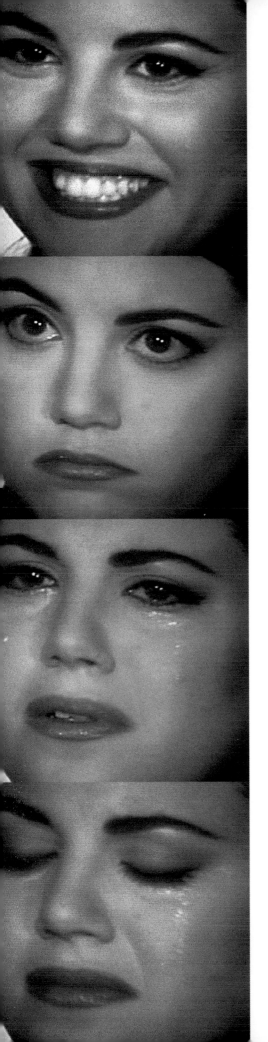

Lewinsky
OPENS UP TO
Walters

Like any good soap opera heroine/victim, she whimpered, she sobbed, she joked—and all the while her lip gloss glistened. In Monica Lewinsky's history-making interview with ABC's Barbara Walters (with 74 million viewers, it was the most-watched TV news program ever, edging out Diane Sawyer's 1995 interview with Michael Jackson and Lisa Marie Presley), the 25-year-old former White House intern/femme fatale was at times surprisingly eloquent, while disturbingly naive at others. And yet what impressed us most—shocked us, really—wasn't her spectrum of emotions, but the fact that she actually came off okay. On TV, "that woman" became a person: Suddenly, we knew all about her abortion, her thoughts of suicide, her desperate wait for phone calls from the guy she was seeing, who just happened to be—*hello!*—the Leader of the Free World. Of course, in keeping with the absurdity of it all, the interview fallout became focused on Lewinsky's lip glosses (among them, Club Monaco's $13 "Glaze"), which became best-sellers the next day. And while Walters was lauded for her gentle-but-forceful interview technique, TV journalism's mother hen still provided late-night talk-show writers with plenty of fodder after asking such befuddled questions as, "What is phone sex?" At least Walters didn't neglect to get the important information: The President "was a good kisser," Lewinsky assured her. And with that, the American people could finally rest.

03.03.99
'PRIVATE' CEREMONIES
Always a reliable Oscar predictor, the Producers Guild of America awards its top honors to *Saving Private Ryan*. Three days later, Steven Spielberg wins the Directors Guild Award.

03.04.99
SPAWN OF SPICE, THE SEQUEL
Brooklyn Joseph Beckham debuts at No. 2 on the "Babies Born to Spice Girls" chart. As for his name, mother Posh (Victoria Adams) notes she was in New York City when she learned of the pregnancy. The borough of Brooklyn is flattered—and a little embarrassed.

03.04.99
BLOW BY BLOW
St. Martin's Press publishes *Monica's Story*, as told to Princess Diana biographer Andrew Morton. Despite the inevitable media frenzy, the book spends only a week at No. 1 before being unseated by George Stephanopoulos' Clinton à clef *All Too Human*.

03.08.99
THE FACE THAT LAUNCHED A THOUSAND HITS
To demonstrate the importance of the Internet, comedian John Byner becomes the first celebrity to broadcast his facelift online. His new mug goes public March 29—again, on the Internet.

03.08.99
SHO 'NUFF
At the annual ShoWest convention in Las Vegas, opening today, the second trailer for *Star Wars: Episode I–The Phantom Menace* takes a backseat to a 90-second preview of *Eyes Wide Shut*, wherein Tom Cruise and Nicole Kidman get kinky in front of a mirror.

03.14.99
VOTER APATHY
It's the Clinton vs. Dole of the Oscar races: A *Los Angeles Times* poll reveals that 61 percent of Americans have not seen even one of this year's Best Picture contenders.

03.15.99
THE LEGENDS HAVE IT
Rock Brahmins Billy Joel, Paul McCartney, Dusty Springfield, and Bruce Springsteen are among those inducted into the Rock and Roll Hall of Fame.

IRE AND ICE Top, Dennehy livens up *Salesman*; Spacey cools his heels in *Iceman*

03.22.99
ODB POLICE BLOTTER (No. 3)
Mr. Bastard returns. The many-monikered rapper is arrested in Brooklyn after a routine traffic stop. A search reveals three bags of—you guessed it—crack cocaine. The case is still pending.

03.23.99
THE POPE CHARTS
The Pope's first album, *Abbà Pater*, drops. The Pontiff mixes old favorites ("Our Father") and new classics (selections from his sermons), underscoring his words with soothing instrumental music. No word on whether he'll tour.

03.24.99
BUY NOW, PAY VADER
Phantom Menace distributor Twentieth Century Fox and Lucasfilm say they will attempt to thwart scalpers by not selling advance tickets for the first two weeks' screenings of the loudly anticipated *Star Wars* prequel. But on April 23 they relent and announce that tickets will go on sale May 12—one week early—with a maximum of 12 per customer.

03.26.99
ODB POLICE BLOTTER (No. 4)
A week after police discovered crack in his vehicle, everybody's favorite Bastard (you know, the Ol' Dirty one) is cited—but, refreshingly, *not* arrested—for driving with a suspended license in Manhattan.

Dennehy and Spacey
HIT THE GREAT WHITE WAY

"Why is it that man desires to be made sad?" a fifth-century thinker once asked. Had he been around to visit Broadway this year, he may well have posed the question again. In an era in which stage shows without music and happy endings often floundered, the end of the millennium saw the return of unapologetic drama. Of course it helped that Kevin Spacey, playing the malevolent Hickey in *The Iceman Cometh*, and Brian Dennehy, who became Willy Loman in *Death of a Salesman*, were the ones leading the way. Indeed, both actors received critical acclaim for their performances in revivals of the old classics (Dennehy won a Tony; Spacey was nominated), but more impressively, both managed to take characters ingrained in our minds and make them different. Spacey—taking over a role widely believed to "belong" to Jason Robards, who starred in *Iceman* in 1956—turned Hickey into a man more hyped up and aggressive, more chilling and opaque than ever before. And Dennehy's monumental frame—not to mention the way he skillfully contrasted that immensity with powerlessness—made the Willy Lomans of the past (including Dustin Hoffman and Lee J. Cobb) seem somehow less significant. While guiding audiences through the darkest corners of man's mind and soul, these actors brought new light to Broadway.

Sean 'Puffy' Combs
TURNS HIMSELF IN

A year ago, Sean "Puffy" Combs was The Man. The acclaimed rapper/producer had his own restaurant and clothing line, a multimillion-dollar East Hampton estate, burgeoning business interests in film and television, and an off-the-hook social schedule. Seemingly, he had the world by the tail. Then came his widely publicized arrest in New York City on April 16 for the alleged beating of record executive Steve Stoute during a dispute about a Nas video, which tucked Combs' own tail firmly between his legs, doing incalculable damage to the upwardly mobile mogul's rep. Combs eventually settled with Stoute and was ordered to attend an anger management class, but the incident made an indelibly negative impression on the public. "The fact that Puffy was in a fight gives him something to write about," joked colleague and Def Jam president Russell Simmons at the time—and indeed Combs used the Stoute affair as fodder for his most recent album, the optimistically titled *Forever*. But the disc's creepily unrepentant mix of gangsta bluster and spiritual posturing apparently turned listeners off, and it slid out of the top 10 in two weeks, spawning no hits. Now, that must have hurt almost as much as the alleged injuries Combs inflicted on Stoute.

COMBS OVER? The rap mogul faces the music after losing his temper

03.30.99
GETTING THE BIRD
In a Hitchcockian turn of events, Fabio is hit in the face by a flying goose while riding the Apollo's Chariot roller coaster at Busch Gardens in Williamsburg, Va. The hunky Italian model, who was promoting the new ride, receives several stitches. The goose is presumed cooked.

04.06.99
CLEAN SLATER
Christian Slater and girlfriend Ryan Haddon give birth to a son, Jaden Christopher. Haddon does most of the work.

04.12.99
END OF THE 'WORLD'
NBC announces It will drop the soap *Another World* on June 25, six weeks after its 35th anniversary. Its replacement, *Passions*, premieres July 5 to dismal reviews but good initial ratings.

04.13.99
STARRY, STARRY SITE
Tefabob Global Enterprises auctions off the domain name *www.maytheforcebe withyou.com* for a whopping $10 million. Suspecting a hoax, e-auctioneer eBay declares the sale void, and the mysterious buyer's e-mail account vanishes. The site remains unsold.

04.14.99
BAIT AND SWITCH
Pamela Anderson Lee says she has removed the implants that supported her trademark D-cup bosom. Some 13 days later, gossip maven Cindy Adams reports that Anderson still has implants: She merely switched from high to low beams.

04.15.99
TRUSTY SPRINGFIELD
The Simpsons is renewed for a 10th season. The show's phenomenal success is considered the driving force behind prime-time TV's animation vogue, spawning hits—and misses—like *King of the Hill*, *The PJs*, *Futurama*, and *Mission Hill*.

04.16.99
'PUBLIC' DOMAIN
Rap group Public Enemy announces plans to make a record available first on the Internet, then in stores. *There's a Poison Goin' On...* is the first release from a major group available exclusively online.

04.16.99
THE WATER BOY
To the delight of the tabloids, Leonardo DiCaprio gets a peek into Davy Jones' locker while filming his upcoming feature *The Beach*. Heavy winds and waves swamp Leo's boat off southern Thailand, forcing the *Titanic* star to jump ship.

04.17.99
BUMMER, CAMP
Avowed shampoo-phobe and MTV VJ Jesse Camp hands his mic over to Thalia DaCosta, a self-styled "starving artist" and winner of the "I Wanna Be a VJ Too" talent search.

04.19.99
SOX APPEAL
Stephen King's *The Girl Who Loved Tom Gordon* debuts at No.1 on the *Publishers Weekly* best-seller list. The meditative thriller—about a young girl who draws inspiration from the heroics of Boston Red Sox reliever Tom Gordon to help her endure a harrowing wilderness adventure—spends 21 weeks on the list.

Tragedy in Littleton
PROVOKES MEDIA SCRUTINY

POP CULT? Manson rants; armed and dangerous in *Killers*; teen rage in *Diaries*

The images are indelibly etched in the country's collective heart and mind: terrified teens fleeing a place they'd believed to be a sanctuary; a boy dropping lifelessly out of a window; a sign with the desperate scrawl "Help...bleeding to death." The senseless tragedy at Columbine High School in Littleton, Colo., may have started out as a front-page story about the 13 killed by Dylan Klebold and Eric Harris, two students on a shooting spree who then turned the guns on themselves, but it ended in a very different place. The event forced us to confront much larger questions: We asked about good and evil, parents and peers, church and state, and that other American institution, pop culture. In the aftermath of blame for Columbine, fingers pointed at the entertainment industry and its growing infatuation with violence: Films like *The Basketball Diaries* and *Natural Born Killers*, and rock acts like Marilyn Manson and Rammstein (Klebold and Harris were apparently fans of the industrial band), were criticized for their perverse influence on youthful fans. But in the end, not much changed. Congressional efforts to abolish First Amendment protection for extremely violent or sexual material and to mandate a government-imposed ratings system failed to win support. Even President Clinton's plea—asking entertainers to make movies they would want their own children to see—had little effect. It didn't matter; by then, every American, whether a parent or not, knew the unspeakable sadness of burying the young.

MOURNING STORY
Memorials to the victims; below, mayhem at the scene; students consoling each other

04.24.99
THE XX FILES
Actress Téa Leoni delivers a daughter, Madelaine West Duchovny. Hubby David doesn't have to look far for the truth—he's the father.

04.24.99
WOODY MAKES ROOM...
Props and tchotchkes from a decade's worth of Woody Allen films are auctioned off at a warehouse in Queens, N.Y. Most of the buyers are not professional collectors, and prices stay low. Bids on Alan Alda are not allowed.

04.25.99
...FOR A NEW ADDITION
The Woodman and wife Soon-Yi Previn tell the *New York Post* they have a daughter, Bechet Dumaine Allen—and that she's already several months old. The couple won't say whether the child was adopted, leaving plenty to the imagination.

04.26.99
MILLENNIALISTS, TAKE NOTE
First the Pope cuts an album, then Sinéad O'Connor is ordained as the first woman priest. O'Connor, whose priesthood is recognized by the obscure Latin Tridentine Church, tells the BBC she's sorry she shredded a photo of the Pope on *Saturday Night Live* seven years earlier.

04.27.99
WORTH THE WAITS
After six years of silence, gravel-throated singer Tom Waits releases *Mule Variations* to positive reviews and respectable sales (especially on college charts).

04.28.99
LOOZIN' IT
Citing an inability to book solid headliners, organizers announce there will be no Lollapalooza '99.

05.05.99
RUNAWAY RATINGS
Viewership of NBC's *Law & Order* skyrockets when Julia Roberts makes an appearance with beau and series regular Benjamin Bratt. Bratt, an apparent believer in term limits, will exit the show at season's end after four years.

05.09.99

NUN'S THE WORD

Critical darling *The Practice* ends its season with a shocker: The final shot reveals George Vogelman (Michael Monks), the nebbishy loner whom Eleanor (Camryn Manheim) had cleared of murder charges, in a nun's habit, indicating he stabbed Eleanor's law partner Lindsay Dole (Kelli Williams).

05.10.99

AMERICA'S SWEETHEART

Amy "The Long Island Lolita" Fisher is released from prison. In 1992, at 17, Fisher pleaded guilty to an assault charge after shooting Mary Jo Buttafuoco, wife of Fisher's paramour Joey Buttafuoco. David Letterman's Top Ten writers breathe a sigh of relief.

05.10.99

PARK PROSPECT

Islands of Adventure becomes the latest attraction at Universal Studios Escape theme park in Orlando, Fla. Creative consultant Steven Spielberg attends the press preview, but conspicuously neglects to warn officials against the dangers of engineering dinosaurs for human amusement.

05.13.99

MODEL STUDENT

Supermodel Christy Turlington graduates from NYU, greatly increasing her chances of finding a job.

JEDI TRICKS Top, Liam Neeson, Jake Lloyd, Ewan McGregor; the madness surrounding *Menace*

The 'Phantom Menace'
PUTS THE HYPE IN HYPERDRIVE

Okay, so the Force is still with us—is anyone surprised? But with the May 19 debut of George Lucas' *Star Wars: Episode I—The Phantom Menace*, it was more than with us: It was all over us like fur on a Wookiee. *Menace* ushered in a new era of movie hype and hysteria: There were tent-dwelling fans queued up in front of theaters weeks in advance, an unprecedented number of related websites, round-the-clock showings, and enough tie-in products to make even Yoda a little dizzy. And though you can still pick a fight by saying Jar Jar Binks wasn't so bad, you can't argue with this: When its box office take hit $400 million, *Phantom Menace* became the third highest-grossing domestic film of all time. Still, there was some distress in the Empire. Because of early galactic predictions (some experts estimated *Menace* would sail past *Titanic*'s $600 million gross), Lucas had to fight a growing perception that the film had not performed up to expectations. Rumors that tie-ins were selling slowly were so pervasive that Hasbro, the biggest maker of *Star Wars* toys, saw its stock dip 30 percent from May (when the movie opened) to August. Yet along with Pepsi, which marketed Queen Amidala and Obi-Wan soda cans, Hasbro reported that sales were out of this world. But the saga is not yet over—two more *Star Wars* prequels will follow in the next few years. So don't throw out your rebel helmets and lightsabers just yet.

Susan Lucci

FINALLY NABS A DAYTIME EMMY

It was a two-decade-long drama capped by that most elusive of soap opera devices: a happy ending. On May 21, before a packed house at New York City's Madison Square Garden and a TV audience of 14 million, Susan Lucci ended one of entertainment's longest losing streaks—18 failed bids in 21 years—by nabbing her first Daytime Emmy for her role as *All My Children*'s man-eating bitch goddess Erica Kane. While insiders had predicted that this was La Lucci's year, thanks to a heart-wrenching story line in which Erica's daughter Bianca struggled with anorexia, the 52-year-old actress seemed genuinely shocked when presenter Shemar Moore (*The Young & the Restless*) proclaimed, "The streak is over—Susan Lucci!" As Lucci put it, "I truly never believed that this would happen." Neither did the crowd, which leapt to its feet—and then booed when producers tried to cut short Lucci's eloquent, unscripted acceptance speech. Through tears, the actress vowed to return to work that week and play Erica for all she was worth. And now, she's worth her weight in gold.

SCHOOL SEX SCANDAL
Asst. principal busted for molesting student **PAGE 9**

VOLPE'S BIG GAMBLE
Torture cop may take stand in own defense **PAGE 6**

NEW YORK POST

SPORTS EXTRA

HOME DELIVERY
1-800-552-7878
CALL TODAY!

http://www.nypost.com/ · · · · 50¢

SATURDAY, MAY 22, 1999 / Cloudy, possible showers, 76-82 / Weather: Page 27 ★

AT LAST!

A beaming Lucci with husband Helmut Huber at Madison Square Garden, where she was named Best Actress for her role on "All My Children."

Susan Lucci snaps 18-year losing streak with 1st Emmy PAGE 3

Mike Tyson wins early parole PAGE 3

The Mob
HITS HOLLYWOOD IN A BIG WAY

Just when we thought we were done with stories about the Mafia...Hollywood *pulled us back in.* Among the Mob tales audiences couldn't refuse this year: HBO's series *The Sopranos*, Robert De Niro's box office hit *Analyze This*, and the Hugh Grant comedy *Mickey Blue Eyes*. But the trend was more than just a goodfella renaissance—it was a reimagining of gangster clichés, dealing less with historical accuracy and more with hysterical consequences. These characters' shady dealings are secondary; the first order of business is funny business, and often at the expense of that once-untouchable archetype, the don. So instead of the powerful patriarch who expounds on the importance of honor—and then orders some low-level goombah whacked—Tony Soprano (the Emmy-nominated James Gandolfini) is literally a "family" man who endures near-crippling bouts of *agita* over his, um, career (which, interestingly, is also how De Niro's Paul Vitti ends up on shrink Billy Crystal's couch in *Analyze This*). And James Caan's Frank Vitale in *Blue Eyes* is such a sweet godfather-in-law that Mickey (Grant) doesn't mind marrying into the Mob for fiancée Gina (Jeanne Tripplehorn). These kinder, gentler capos are the sort of made men that '90s audiences could cuddle up to—without any fear of sleeping with the fishes.

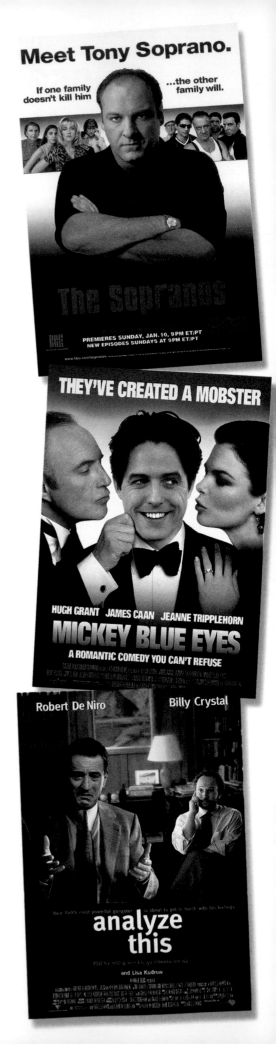

Season Finales
THAT KEPT US DANGLING

For a while, it seemed as if the season-ending cliff-hanger—the kind that left viewers wailing "Three months till I find out what happens?"—had gone the way of rabbit ears. Then, in May, NBC's *Friends* and The WB's *Felicity* revived the practice with two extraordinary finales. *Friends* pulled the ultimate fake-out: Monica and Chandler go to a Vegas wedding chapel, only to find an inebriated Ross and Rachel leaving—as husband and wife. Meanwhile, in another part of New York City, Felicity was pondering a hunk conundrum: fly to Berlin with sensitive Noel or take a road trip with broody Ben? But before we learned where her taxi was headed, the credits rolled. Not since J.R. lay shot on his office floor in 1980 had viewers been left on such prime-time pins and needles. And the CIA-strength security around the plots made the payoffs more effective. Even Scott Speedman, *Felicity*'s Ben, had to wait it out: "I asked the pro-

ducers," he told EW, "but they wouldn't tell me." Fall couldn't come soon enough: Twenty-seven million tuned in to see Ross and Rachel's morning-after realization (they've spent much of the season trying to get the boozy union annulled), while 4.7 million finally learned of Felicity's choice: It was Ben (at least for a few episodes; they soon broke up). Such satisfying examples of delayed gratification will no doubt lead to more TV waiting games in 2000.

HANGERS-ON *Felicity*'s Scott Foley (above left) and Speedman; *Friends*' Jennifer Aniston and David Schwimmer are knot worthy

06.06.99
STAGE DIVE
The Tony Awards air on CBS, shorn of veteran emcee Rosie O'Donnell. The Queen of Nice—who had declined to host but was planning an appearance—withdrew altogether after a caller on *Howard Stern* threatened her son. Ratings indicate a 2.5-million-viewer drop-off from last year's Tonys.

06.09.99
U-TURN
Director Oliver Stone is in the clink for a suspected DWI and possession of hashish; he's released the next day on $12,500 bail. On Aug. 24 Stone announces a tentative plea bargain: two misdemeanor charges, rehab...and a solemn promise to make fewer trippy montage sequences.

06.11.99
ROCKIN' FELLER
Ricky Martin makes *vida* a wee bit *loca* by performing live on the *Today* show at Rockefeller Center in New York City. His fabled gyrations draw a screaming assemblage and record crowds for *Today*.

06.12.99
RHETT CONTROL
Michael Jackson takes home his first Oscar; unfortunately, it's the one awarded to David O. Selznick for 1939's Best Picture, *Gone With the Wind*. The $1.2 million sale occurs at an auction in New York City, where Jacko is recording his latest album.

06.12.99
FRIENDLY MATCH
Must-See veteran Courteney Cox and frenzied 1-800-CALL-ATT pitchman David Arquette are wed in San Francisco. The pair met on the set of 1996's *Scream*. Historians take note: The "Courteney Cox Arquette" epoch will soon begin.

06.16.99
APE IS ENOUGH
There's a rumble in the Tinseltown jungle, and it's *Tarzan*, Disney's highest-grossing movie since *The Lion King*. With a chest-pounding $110 million plus in just three weeks, the Edgar Rice Burroughs warhorse proves a critical and financial smash.

06.19.99
BARELY REGAL
Prince–cum–TV producer Edward Windsor of Britain weds commoner–cum–PR exec Sophie Rhys-Jones in a relatively casual ceremony at St. George's Cathedral. The BBC has exclusive broadcasting rights to the event, and 200 million tune in to see the happy couple seal their vows—without a kiss.

06.23.99
DAD ON ARRIVAL
Dharma & Greg's Thomas Gibson (he's the Greg half) and wife Cristina welcome their first son, James Parker, in Los Angeles.

06.24.99
STRINGS ATTACHED
Brownie, the electric guitar Eric Clapton used to write *Layla*, fetches $497,500, the highest sum ever paid at auction for a guitar. Christie's moves a total of 100 Clapton axes, generating more than $5 million for the artist's rehab center (conveniently located in Antigua).

06.29.99
ET TU, TOUPEE?
NBC ends the backbiting and rehires mighty-mouthed sportscaster Marv Albert. The net axed him in 1997 after he entered a guilty plea to a misdemeanor assault charge (part of a bargain to avoid more serious forcible-sodomy charges) in a humiliating suit brought by a longtime lover.

06.30.99
LIVIN' LARGE
Camryn Manheim, Emmy-winning star of ABC's *The Practice*, models plus-sizes for Lane Bryant's Venezia collection at the Hammerstein Ballroom in New York City. "This is for all the fashionable girls!"

LOST HOPE From top: Notes of loss; tears in New York City; the search efforts; the couple sets sail

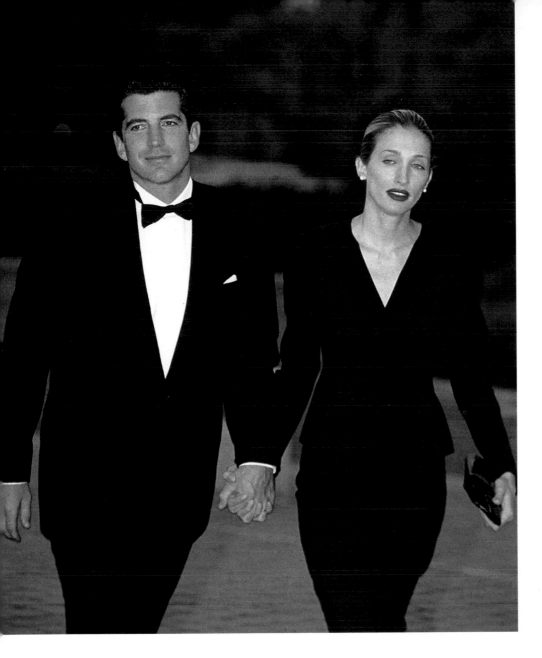

JFK Jr.'s Plane Crashes
AND AMERICA MOURNS

The news crept out slowly: John F. Kennedy Jr.'s single-engine plane, carrying him, his wife, Carolyn Bessette Kennedy, and her sister Lauren, had disappeared off the coast of Martha's Vineyard on the eve of July 16. Misty-eyed news anchors delivering the few known details—there was a blinding haze, Kennedy was piloting his own Piper Saratoga, the couple was en route to cousin Rory Kennedy's wedding—struggled to refer to the presumed victims in the present tense. But after decades of immersing our imagination in the Kennedy clan's lavish lives, we knew that tragedy was always just a terrible step away. Its claim on JFK Jr.'s

short life (he was 38) was particularly hard to take. After all, this was America's First Child, the boy who grew up before our eyes. We watched as he was christened, yanked on his mother's pearls, and ran across the White House lawn for a hug from his dad, the President. Then we watched as he raised a tiny arm to salute his father's coffin. On the weekend of his death, silvery images from John-John's life—along with shots of the endless search efforts and reports from the impromptu memorial at the couple's Manhattan loft—paraded nonstop across TV screens, ghostly salutes to the nation's golden boy now gone.

07.02.99
GERBER BABY

With hubby/restaurateur Rande Gerber at her side (as well as a nurse and midwife), supermodel and home-birth practitioner Cindy Crawford continues the red-hot "unwieldy name" trend (see "Spawn of Spice") by tagging her newborn son Presley Walker Gerber.

07.04.99
BAD RECEPTION

Speaking of Spice: Posh (a.k.a. Victoria Adams) gets hitched to soccer star David Beckham in a ceremony at Luttrellstown Castle, near Dublin. Some guests celebrate by allegedly pocketing 75 rented silver goblets, which Posh later says were "quite valuable."

07.05.99
RHYTHM INFLATION

Pollstar magazine reports the average price of a concert ticket is up $5 from 1998 and $13 from 1996. Luciano Pavarotti (natch) had the biggest per-seat average, $130.77; the Rolling Stones clocked the second highest—$109.62—most of which will go toward the band's stash of spare livers.

07.07.99
KATZ FIGHT

If Michael Eisner hated Jeffrey Katzenberg before, imagine how he feels after Katzenberg—ex-head of Disney studios and Eisner's favorite "little midget"—pockets a reported $250–275 million settlement. The decision ends a three-year battle, which began when Katzenberg claimed that Disney withheld his film royalties after he quit to start up rival studio DreamWorks.

07.08.99
'ZINE QUEEN

Oprah Winfrey moves one step closer to world domination with the announcement of her new magazine (as yet untitled), which will dedicate itself to a number of female-oriented topics—among them family, spirituality, and the pursuit of nonfat waffles. The magazine is set to debut in the spring of 2000.

07.09.99
GETTING SATISFACTION

Mick Jagger and Jerry Hall agree to annul their tumultuous nine-year marriage, heading off divorce proceedings Hall began in January, when Brazilian model Luciana Morad claimed to be carrying Jagger's child. On July 27, it's announced that a blood test proves that the 56-year-old Rolling Stone is indeed the father.

07.12.99
SUBLIME RICKY

Tickets to an Oct. 28 Ricky Martin concert at Madison Square Garden sell out in just 14 minutes. Martin's Oct. 29 bon-bon-shaking bonanza takes six additional minutes to sell out, making some speculate that his popularity is declining.

07.13.99
RUMBLE IN THE GUMBEL

CBS announces that *This Morning* will become *The Early Show*, as new host Bryant Gumbel prepares to go toe-to-toe with his ex-employer NBC's *Today*, home of his a.m.-show nemesis Katie Couric.

07.14.99
TOM, SAWYER

Diane Sawyer interviews Tom Cruise on both ABC's *Good Morning America* and *20/20*; he discusses *Eyes Wide Shut* and life with Nicole Kidman. Two days later, Sawyer talks to Kidman on *Good Morning America*.

Bruce Springsteen
TOURS WITH THE E STREET BAND

Bruce Springsteen, 50, may be older than rock & roll, but he's in better shape. Witness his summer muscle: While bubblegum pop dominated the charts, the Boss' reunion tour—which paired Springsteen with his old Asbury Park, N.J., posse the E Street Band—became more than a hot ticket. It took on mythic proportions. The first 33 American dates (the tour originated in Barcelona, Spain) sold out with lightning speed. Thankfully, the show delivered on its promise: two hours and 40 minutes of intermission-free, stoked-up, unleashed Bruce. Even the band—his wife, guitarist, and backup singer Patti Scialfa, guitarist Steve Van Zandt, drummer Max Weinberg, keyboardist Roy Bittan, bassist Garry Tallent, and, of course, the big man, saxophonist Clarence Clemons—sounded better than ever. Maybe because this time they were on a mission. "I'm here tonight to rededicate you," Springsteen roared from the stage at one of his 15 New Jersey performances, "to the power, the magic, the mystery, the ministry of rock & roll...." And he did.

Eyes Wide Shut
OPENS AFTER A PROLONGED TEASE

This summer, everyone was sure *Eyes* would have it. The arrival of Stanley Kubrick's erotic opus *Eyes Wide Shut* wasn't only one of the year's most anticipated moments but also one that generated the most gossip. "A story of jealousy and sexual obsession" was all that Warner Bros. would reveal when describing the Tom Cruise–Nicole Kidman project, which shot for a seemingly endless 15 months at a high-security set in London. Naturally, the hush-hush treatment put the rumor mill into even higher gear. (Some choice tidbits: Cruise and Kidman were psychiatrists sexually involved with their patients, and Cruise was in drag during one scene.) Turned out that the rumors were just that. But in the end, it was all anticlimactic. Kubrick's intellectual take on sex was more deep thoughts than *Deep Throat* and compromised the box office clout of the stars. While *Eyes* overcame mostly mediocre reviews and opened strong (with a $21.7 first-weekend take), the film soon fizzled, a victim—ironically—of bad word of mouth.

YOU GO, BOSS Above, Springsteen rocks with Nils Lofgren (left) and Van Zandt; below, Bruce fans are purple with pleasure. Opposite, Kidman and Cruise shut their *Eyes*

07.15.99
BETWEEN BROS.
Bob Daly and Terry Semel, one of Hollywood's longest-running management teams, resign as cochairmen of Warner Bros. On Aug. 2, Time Warner names former studio chief operating officer Barry Meyer the new chairman and chief executive officer, with Alan Horn serving as president and COO. It's believed their first executive act will be the ritualistic burning of *Wild Wild West*.

07.16.99
HUNT'S OVER
Helen Hunt marries longtime beau (and *Simpsons* voice of all trades) Hank Azaria this weekend in Los Angeles. It is widely assumed that they are "mad about" each other.

07.16.99
LASS DISMISSED
In a resounding defeat for quality television, Roseanne's gabfest, which debuted in September 1998, is pulled from NBC's local stations—the death knell for a syndicated talk show. Soon even Tom Arnold may be declining guest appearances.

07.26.99
GERE MADNESS
Hoary hunk Richard Gere stamps his hand- and footprints in the famous forecourt of Mann's Chinese Theatre. In November, he'll be named Sexiest Man Alive by PEOPLE. Jeez, was *Runaway Bride* that good?

07.31.99
ODB POLICE BLOTTER (No. 5)
Miss him? After almost three arrest-free months, El Bastardo Sordido Anciano is back, as he runs a red light in Queens, N.Y. A search of his Bastardmobile allegedly reveals 20 envelopes of crack cocaine. Charges have not been filed.

08.02.99
EDITRIX OF THE TRADE
Riding a tidal wave of hype, editor extraordinaire Tina Brown unveils *Talk*, her Miramax Films-backed general-interest magazine, at a star-studded launch party held at New York's Statue of Liberty.

08.03.99
"CREEK" HERO
Dawson's Creek star Joshua Jackson pulls a Tom Cruise, braving the surf off Wrightsville Beach, N.C., where the show is filmed, to aid two floundering female swimmers. Jackson and a friend reach the victims—but are themselves caught in the current. All are saved by the Coast Guard. Teen girls everywhere swoon.

08.10.99
NO GUTS, NO GLORY
Carnie Wilson, daughter of music guru and former Beach Boy Brian Wilson, undergoes gastric bypass surgery on a live webcast. The procedure is an effort to combat obesity. The webcast is an effort to nauseate us all.

08.11.99
PREZ CORPS
Warren Beatty hints at a run for President in 2000 and starts a trend: Cybill Shepherd is soon said to be considering a run, and real estate tycoon Donald Trump surfaces in September as a Reform Party candidate, riding on the boa of supporter Jesse Ventura.

08.11.99
TONGUE STUDS
Metal-makeup rockers Kiss get a star on the Hollywood Walk of Fame, despite their celluloid sin *Detroit Rock City*.

TAKING 'STOCK
Clockwise from top, A mosh-pit diver goes deep; Jewel provides a serene moment; Kid Rock lets the fur fly; the grounds heat up

Woodstock
GOES UP IN FLAMES

If peace and love were the bywords of the original Woodstock, its 1999 descendant subverted those hippie platitudes as rudely as did the Clash in their 1977 punk classic "Hate and War." Sure, there was some good music to be heard over those three hot summer days (July 23–25) at Griffiss Park, a former Air Force base in Rome, N.Y., where the event was held. But between the $4 bottled water, the roving bands of boys intent on violating as many women as possible, the war-zone feel of the surroundings, and the knuckleheads who rioted, looted, and set fires on the festival's final night, who can really summon up any positive feelings about the debacle? "I believe that the overwhelming majority of kids were there simply to enjoy the music and have a good time, and the troublemakers in attendance amounted to far, far less than one percent of the crowd," said promoter John Scher after the event, and he may be right (though there's no real way to check his math). Nonetheless, Woodstock 99's legacy is a grim one. The concert's aftermath brought a deluge of speculation about who was ultimately responsible for the violence. The promoters? The kids? The drugs? The bands? Some cosmic plague of bad vibes? In the end, perhaps MTV commentator Kurt Loder had the most cogent take on the whole depressing affair. "It's like any disaster," he told EW at the time. "There's plenty of blame to go around."

08.12.99
TOUCH MY MONEY
Mike Myers, in the wake of the smash *Austin Powers* sequel, eyes a $20 million deal to play German talk-show host Dieter in the film of *Sprockets*, a Myers skit from *Saturday Night Live*. *Goat Boy: The Movie* is now inevitable.

08.14.99
THE NEW-HEART SHOW
At a private party in Orlando, Fla., Elton John gives his first performance since getting a pacemaker. He's still standing.

08.16.99
WHAT'S THE CO-PAYMENT?
Daily Variety reports that *ER*'s producers will pay Eriq La Salle $27 million to remain as Dr. Peter Benton for three more years—another sign that the show is bleeding stars after George Clooney's high-profile exit. In November, Julianna Margulies (Nurse Hathaway) will turn down $27 million to return for two years.

08.21.99
OFF THE MARK
At the archery semifinals in Bloomfield, N.J., actress/Olympic hopeful Geena Davis loses her bid to shoot with the U.S. team at the 2000 Sydney games. Now she can aim for a new career.

08.24.99
WHAT'S THE BUZZ?
Access Hollywood airs the first footage of *Felicity* star Keri Russell shorn of her trademark long curls. The horror! The horror!

08.27.99
BENIGNI THERE, DONE THAT
Miramax Films is living *la dolce vita*, thanks to an additional $353,000 in ticket revenue with the English-dubbed rerelease of its Oscar-winning Holocaust fable, *Life is Beautiful*. Final tally: $57.6 million.

09.01.99
SAM'S CLUB
Sam Donaldson announces that he's leaving ABC News' White House beat and, beginning Sept. 27, will host a 15-minute news report that will be seen thrice weekly on ABCNEWS.com. That'll keep kids off the Net.

09.12.99
LOOKS LIKE A RERUN

The *51st Annual Emmy Awards* goes blandly where many Emmys have gone before: bad shtick, familiar winners (*NYPD Blue*'s Dennis Franz *again*?), and shafted newcomers (*The Sopranos*). It's the lowest-rated Emmys in a decade.

09.14.99
GOING DUCHESS

NBC's *Today* show gives itself the royal treatment by hiring ex-duchess and dieter Sarah Ferguson as a special correspondent. She'll do human-interest stories, interviews...all the weighty issues.

09.14.99
CROW'S FEAT

American Express sponsors "Sheryl Crow and Friends," a free show in Central Park. The "friends" are Sarah McLachlan, the Dixie Chicks, Chrissie Hynde, Stevie Nicks, Keith Richards, and Eric Clapton, who is considered the group's Chandler.

09.21.99
CHANGE OF HEATHER

ABC's *Spin City* introduces platinum bombshell (and *Melrose Place* refugee) Heather Locklear as a foil for Michael J. Fox's cocksure deputy mayor. The outlandish gamble pays off, and *City* gets some positive buzz. Whodathunkit?

09.21.99
A TOY LIKE THAT

After a customer complains, Sears halts the sale of a Columbine-esque action figure that appears in its 1999 Wish Book catalog. The adorable poppet comes complete with ski mask, black trench coat, body armor, shotgun, and rifle. Media frenzy not included.

'The Sixth Sense'
SCARES UP A TON OF BUSINESS

In a year that embraced all things spooky (from *The Blair Witch Project* to *House on Haunted Hill* to *The Bone Collector*), *The Sixth Sense* seemed, at first, just another ghost story. But like an apparition floating in out of nowhere, the film—with its oddly hopeful take on the afterlife and a twist ending that kept audiences entranced through repeated viewings—turned into a sleeper hit. It topped the box office charts for five weeks, took in more than $270 million, and catapulted young actor Haley Joel Osment and writer-director M. Night Shyamalan into that otherworldly realm of Hollywood A-listers. Star Bruce Willis, meanwhile, experienced a career resurrection beyond his big-budget action meal tickets (he's agreed to star in Shyamalan's next film *Unbreakable*). And what sense did Hollywood make of *Sense*? Based on the success of the movie's whispered tag line ("I see dead people"), expect to see similarly subtle marketing tactics, as well as a spate of good old-fashioned fright nights coming soon to a theater near you. But if that means better movies, then bring out the dead.

'Austin Powers'
BREAKS $200 MILLION

A movie about the poached mojo of a dentally challenged man of mystery almost overshadowed *Phantom Menace*? Give us a frickin' break! Opening to record crowds on June 11, *Austin Powers: The Spy Who Shagged Me* nearly quadrupled the take of its spy-spoofing '97 original. By mid-August, Mike Myers' swingin' sequel had shagged its way to more than...*$200 meeellion dollars* at the box office, becoming a welcome blockbuster for New Line studios and one of the top-grossing films of summer. Not to mention one of the most ubiquitous. While Mr. Bigglesworth dolls and etched martini glasses flew off store shelves, Austin and his furry chest could be seen endorsing everything from airlines to milk, and the irresistible catchphrase "shagadelic" was as big as Fat Bastard. But it was the little things that meant a lot—as in 32-inch costar Verne Troyer, who, as Dr. Evil's tiny clone Mini-Me, was the perfect counterpart to Austin's pinkie-nibbling nemesis. (As Evil himself noted, "You complete me.") Funny thing is, no one expected Austin to have such big-screen powers—not even the director, Jay Roach. "We honestly thought we were making a movie for our friends," he told EW. "Any conversations we had about doing a sequel were part of a big inside joke." So, will the switched-on secret agent be back for a third trip? Our guess is, "Yeah, baby!"

09.22.99
TIT FOR TAT
Stopped in the name of Heathrow Airport security (for setting off a metal detector), Diana Ross angrily gropes a British officer's breast after a body search. The diva is busted for the retributive squeeze and then released with a warning.

09.24.99
DOWNS, HE GOES
Anchor Hugh Downs uses his final *20/20* broadcast to stump for marijuana legalization, which he supports. Thus ends years of speculation surrounding Downs' uncannily relaxed on-air demeanor.

09.27.99
A STAR IS STUDDED
How nice should you be to your ex? Not this nice: Still-hopeful ex-beau Ben Affleck reportedly gave Gwyneth Paltrow diamond studs from Harry Winston for her 27th birthday. With an ex like him, who needs a boyfriend?

09.27.99
FOR LOVE OF THE GLOVE
Rabid Yankee fan and *Analyze This* star Billy Crystal shells out $215,000 for one of Mickey Mantle's old baseball gloves, without even popping into Sotheby's dressing room to see if it fits.

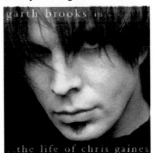

09.28.99
YOU CAN LEAVE YOUR HAT ON
Garth Brooks pulls a Ziggy Stardust, assuming the persona of shaggy, Aussie-born pop crooner Chris Gaines as his new album, *Garth Brooks in...the Life of Chris Gaines*, hits stores. Fans and critics are not pleased, and Brooks wins his battle with schizophrenia by year's end.

09.28.99
HART TARGET
Melissa Joan Hart, who plays the, er, titular role in *Sabrina, the Teenage Witch*, comes under fire for appearing in very skimpy, very non-TGIF attire on the covers of *Maxim* and *Bikini*, thus jeopardizing the wholesome image of her Archie comics character. Hart makes no public apologies. Shameless *witch*!

09.30.99
DUDLEY'S DILEMMA
Beloved *Arthur* star Dudley Moore reveals that he's suffering from PSP, a rare and incurable Parkinson's-like brain disorder that affects his equilibrium and slurs his speech. In November, the star appears on *20/20* to talk about his illness.

09.30.99
TEUTONIC ACHIEVEMENT
Germany's Günter Grass, author of *The Tin Drum*, wins the Nobel Prize in Literature. Oh, they'll give it to anyone with an umlaut in his name.

10.07.99
SECOND HONEYMOON (VIDEO)?
The *New York Daily News* reports that Pamela Anderson Lee and Tommy Lee will remarry—in the nude—on New Year's Eve. Pam's rep can only confirm that they're engaged. Much of America can confirm what they look like naked.

10.08.99
THEY'RE HIStory
Debbie Rowe Jackson, the longtime friend who agreed to bear Michael Jackson's two children, files for divorce, taking the first steps toward making their estrangement legal. The wedded bliss lasted three years—16 months longer than Jacko's first marriage to Lisa Marie Presley. So he's improving.

SIGNS OF THE TIMES Clockwise from top right, John Goodman and Crystal; Molly Shannon goofs with Drew Barrymore; Mike Myers and David Spade; Chris Kattan, Lovitz, and Hanks mug it up

'Saturday Night Live'
CELEBRATES 25 YEARS ON THE AIR

As Billy Crystal's hyper-accented Fernando might say, they looked mah-velous! *Saturday Night Live: The 25th Anniversary Special* not only attracted a star-studded audience of ex-*SNL* regulars (except for no-show Eddie Murphy), former hosts (including Tom Hanks, Michael Douglas, and Jerry Seinfeld), and past musical guests (the Eurythmics performed on the show, and Aerosmith's Steven Tyler rocked at the after-party held at the Rainbow Room), but it was also a ratings smash. Drawing more viewers than any other NBC special since 1993 (22.2 million people tuned in), the three-hour reunion was a veritable nostalgia-fest: Bill Murray reprised his sleazy lounge-singer act; Crystal's Fernando reminded us all that "it is better to look good than to feel good"; and Chevy Chase, Dennis Miller, and Norm Macdonald staged one wickedly funny three-way "Weekend Update." But it wasn't all laughs: The show also featured touching tributes to late cast members Gilda Radner, John Belushi, and Chris Farley, and Jon Lovitz struggled to hold back tears as he introduced a short video in honor of his friend Phil Hartman. Still, the evening provided a glittering glance at some of the best comedy of the past quarter century. When *SNL* first aired, its ensemble of comics were deemed "Not Ready for Prime Time." This special finally proved otherwise.

Grown-Ups
GET A LIFE OF THEIR OWN IN POP CULTURE

It was the season of midlife-crisis chic. While the summer's hot demographic was nubile teens, by fall a cool new trend had emerged: grown-ups on TV. After several years of *Friends*-like twentysomethings and hormone-driven high schoolers dominating the prime-time slots, the over-40 set staged a victorious comeback. ABC's *Once and Again*, starring Sela Ward and Billy Campbell as a newly separated mom and a divorced dad, was hailed by critics and viewers alike, providing the network with its highest-rated drama premiere since 1995's *Murder One*. CBS' *Family Law*, starring Kathleen Quinlan as a suddenly single attorney opening a law practice on a shoe-string budget, has won its time slot since it debuted in September. And CBS' *Judging Amy* attracted viewers to the trials and tribulations of a woman (Amy Brenneman) balancing family and career. The effort to reflect the midlife experience even went beyond the small screen: Not only was *American Beauty*—about fortysomethings questioning their suburban existence—one of the year's most buzzed-about movies, but *The Thomas Crown Affair* featured Pierce Brosnan romancing a fortyish—and topless—Rene Russo. Who says growing up isn't fun?

ADULT THEMES Left, *Amy*'s Brenneman and Richard T. Jones; above, *Now*'s Ward and Campbell; *Law*'s Quinlan approaches the bench

10.11.99
IN-THE-RED PLANET
Glitz-themed, debt-laden eatery chain Planet Hollywood says it will close nine of its 32 U.S. locations. The next day, it files for bankruptcy. This despite backers like Bruce Willis and Arnold Schwarzenegger, not to mention some damn fine overpriced hamburgers.

10.12.99
TRAVELING PILLSBURYS
Aging, zaftig bards Crosby, Stills, Nash & Young say they'll tour to promote their new album, *Looking Forward*. This marks the full group's only collaborative effort since 1988's *American Dream*, their first tour in 25 years, and the debut of Crosby's second liver.

10.14.99
'HOPE' ALSO FLOATS
On David E. Kelley's *Chicago Hope*, Dr. Jack McNeil (Mark Harmon) says "s--- happens." It's the first time the excremental word is used on a network show. Some affiliates bleep it out. The nation breathlessly waits to see how *Touched by an Angel* will top that.

10.14.99
ALDA RAGE
Meanwhile, still in Chicago, at County General, Alan Alda begins a stint on *ER* as Dr. Lawrence, a renowned physician with a lot of pride—and Alzheimer's. He doesn't even remember he used to be called Hawkeye Pierce.

10.16.99
STRUNG OUT
Yo-Yo Ma leaves his 266-year-old cello in the trunk of a New York City cab. Using Ma's receipt, police and some Taxi & Limousine Commission folks are able to track down the cab and reunite the priceless instrument with its anxious owner.

10.19.99
A VERY GOOD 'LIVING'
It's a "bull" Martha at the New York Stock Exchange as shares of Martha Stewart Living Omnimedia Inc. debut at $18 and close at $35.56. Martha madness levels off after a few days, and shares stabilize around $30, but the NYSE discovers it can make great fall decorations from ticker tape.

10.21.99
SPOTTED 'FEVER'

Fresh from a lucrative London debut, *Saturday Night Fever*, a stage musical adapted from the 1977 John Travolta sensation, opens on Broadway to derisive reviews. But over $20 million in advance ticket sales ensures that it will indeed be stayin' alive for a while.

10.22.99
DISSED JOCKEY

It's announced that shock jock Howard Stern and his wife, Alison, are separating after 21 years of marriage. Stern takes most of the blame, saying his "workaholic" nature put stress on the relationship. Stern is expected to ask his friends in the porn industry for guidance.

10.27.99
BUT IT *WASN'T* FROM THE GAP

The dress Marilyn Monroe wore while singing "Happy Birthday" to President John F. Kennedy in 1962 is auctioned for $1,267,500 at Christie's. The lucky recipient isn't Ken Starr, but rather the team of Robert Schagrin and Peter Siegel, owners of a New York City collectibles company.

10.28.99
RUSHDIE JUDGMENT

An Islamic fatwa—or "judicial opinion"—is placed on Tony-winning playwright Terrence McNally when his *Corpus Christi* hits the London stage. In the play, Jesus, considered an important prophet by Muslims, engages in gay sex. A fatwa is viewed by many as a death sentence—and by many others as free publicity.

Sometimes life doesn't imitate art. And that became all too clear when the news broke that 45-year-old Jerry Seinfeld—who had turned dumping girlfriends into an art form for nine seasons on his hit sitcom—had popped the question to his real-life uptown girl, Jessica Sklar, 28. A publicist for designer Tommy Hilfiger, Sklar scandalously ended her marriage to Broadway theater scion Eric Nederlander just weeks after their honeymoon in order to date the comedian. And just about everything about the engagement was as New York City-centric as you would imagine Seinfeld to be. The couple, who reportedly met at the Reebok Sports Club near his Upper West Side apartment, became engaged at Balthazar, a fashionable downtown Manhattan bistro, and bought the ring at Tiffany's on Fifth Avenue—a series of events that would certainly discombobulate the four nitpicky New Yorkers on *Seinfeld*, with their major "commitment issues." (In fact, since he's been famous, Jerry's only had one other serious girlfriend: Shoshanna Lonstein, whom he started seeing when she was 17.) No wedding date was announced, but the ceremony is expected to be small and intimate. Now, *that* won't be an event about nothing.

TAKE MY WIFE, PLEASE Seinfeld, bachelorhood's poster boy, shocked many by proposing to Sklar

'Pokémon' & 'Toy Story 2'
ROUND UP MOVIEGOING KIDS

It *is* a small world after all. At least it seemed that way in November, when kid power helped break box office records. On Nov. 10, it was *Pokémon: The First Movie*, based on the Japanese multimedia empire that includes videogames, a top-rated TV series, toys, and addictive trading cards. The movie grossed $50.8 million in five days and became the biggest Wednesday opening for an animated film. (It also sparked an outbreak of "Pokémon flu," as thousands of kids skipped school to see it.) Never mind that many of us still don't know a Pikachu from a Meowth. Later in the month, Disney marched out the Pixar-animated *Toy Story 2*, which earned a plush $80.5 million over the five-day Thanksgiving holiday. The megaplex appeal of both movies wasn't that surprising, really: Earlier in the year, *Pokémon*'s menagerie of monsters had morphed into the mother of all kiddie crazes, with the trading cards alone racking up about $300 million in sales. *Toy Story 2* was one of the most anticipated movies of the year (think *The Godfather Part II* of animation), and is expected to earn more than $200 million, the second Disney release this year to reach such heights (*The Sixth Sense* is the other.) That's what we call living happily ever after.

YEAR IN REVIEW

11.19.99
WE HAVE A WIENER

After nearly an hour of perceived smugness, Connecticut IRS investigator John Carpenter becomes the first $1 million winner on *Who Wants to Be a Millionaire*. "I sort of expected to win," says Carpenter. Who wants to see him soaked by his employer?

11.21.99
READY TO ROCK?

Brad Pitt appears to be taking another step toward making an honest woman of Jennifer Aniston when the pair show off her diamond ring at a Sting concert in New York City. Pitt's spokeswoman later says it was a joke. And quite a hilarious one at that.

11.28.99
THE RAPTURE

After seeing how a forbidden kiss reinvigorated *Ally McBeal*, Mulder and Scully try a similar maneuver on *The X-Files*. It's the platonic pair's first "real" kiss in the show's seven-season history. Seas do not boil. Skies do not fall.

11.30.99
SCOUT'S HONOR

England's Scout Association blasts Elton John for including male strippers dressed as Boy Scouts in his performance at a gay rights benefit. This may frustrate John's ambition to become a troop leader.

Jennifer Lopez
INSURES HER BOOTY FOR $1 BILLION

Getting to the bottom of celebrity gossip isn't always easy. And getting the truth about Jennifer Lopez's bottom can prove equally difficult. Which is why folks blinked when the *New York Post*'s front page pronounced Lopez a "billion-dollar babe" after the actress allegedly took out a $1 billion insurance policy on her body. At first, it made sense. After all, the 29-year-old Bronx bombshell's appeal lies as much in her bodacious bod and her ample derriere as it does in her acting and singing. And certainly, she wasn't the first celebrity to place such a premium on her, uh, talent: Onetime pinup queen Betty Grable, Marlene Dietrich, and hoofer Fred Astaire all famously had insurance policies covering their legs (Elizabeth Taylor even had one for her eyes). And a day after the report, which the *Post* had picked up from the London *Sun*, Sharon Stone told an *Access Hollywood* reporter that she has a body insurance policy—though she declined to reveal for how much. Still, as often happens in the dish industry, the Lopez report turned out to be false. Lopez's publicist Alan Nierob insisted "they made the whole thing up. We don't know anything about her taking out any insurance policy." Nevertheless, the story did propel Lopez into the headlines. Guess that's the bottom line.

TAKING AIM *The Green Mile* (top), *Angela's Ashes* (left), and *Beauty* were Oscar hopefuls

The Oscar Race Begins

MOVIES GO FOR THE GOLD

There are certain things you can count on as December winds down: chestnuts will be roasting, Martha Stewart will be hand-painting wrapping paper—and the Oscar race kicking into high gear. The Christmas season is traditionally a time when the studios roll out their "serious" contenders, and 1999 was no exception. By the end of summer, only *The Sixth Sense*'s Haley Joel Osment and its writer-director, M. Night Shyamalan, had the momentum to make more than a few shortlists. September's *American Beauty*—with its juicy turns from Kevin Spacey, Annette Bening, and newcomer Wes Bentley—and November's Michael Mann-directed *The Insider* were the kind of edgy dramas that impress the Academy. Then the calendar's final weeks separated the big gifts from the stocking stuffers, there was the somber memoir *Angela's Ashes*, the period drama *Anna and the King*, the thriller *The Talented Mr. Ripley*, the anticipated biopic *Man on the Moon*, plus a talked-about turn from the actor Oscar loves most: Tom Hanks in *The Green Mile*. Of course, who will actually get the gold remains—well, it remains the best watercooler conversation for at least a few more months. So, until next year…

12.07.99
FOSTERING DISCUSSION
For the first time, Jodie Foster speaks in depth to a reporter (*60 Minutes II*'s Charlie Rose) about John Hinckley's assassination attempt on Ronald Reagan, which Hinckley said was an attempt to get Foster's attention. The actress confirms that it did indeed get her attention.

12.08.99
SEALING 'BEAUTY'
The National Board of Review names *American Beauty* '99's Best Film. However, this decision was made before the debut of *Deuce Bigalow: Male Gigolo*.

12.09.99
SEAMUS PROMOTION
The New York *Daily News* reports that Woody Allen's estranged 11-year-old son Satchel is attending Simon's Rock College in Great Barrington, Mass., and applying for admission to New York City's Columbia University next fall. The wunderkind's smartest move to date: going by the name Seamus Farrow.

12.14.99
COMIC RELIEVED
Peanuts creator Charles Schulz, 77, announces he will retire from drawing the popular 50-year-old comic strip in order to focus on his battle with colon cancer. His last original strip featuring Charlie Brown, Snoopy, and the gang is slated to run Feb. 6. Rats!

12.17.99
WAXY BUILDUP
Madame Tussaud's Rock Circus unveils wax casts of the Spice Girls (minus Geri Halliwell), the first band molded since the Beatles. The girls will remain inside the casts until their careers revive.

← EXCEPTIONAL FEET Debra Messing and Eric McCormack polished off another season of *Will & Grace* (photograph by Robert Trachtenberg)

↑ HUGE GRANT The dapper Hugh was bigger than ever after lighting up movie screens in *Notting Hill* (photograph by Lorenzo Agius)

↑ STUD MUFFIN The WWF's Gangrel was one of the stars of wrestling who body-slammed pop culture (photograph by Mary Ellen Mark)

→ CAUGHT IN *ACTION* Buddy Hackett, Illeana Douglas, and Jay Mohr dream of better days—Fox's acidic inside-Hollywood show was canceled (photograph by Dan Winters)

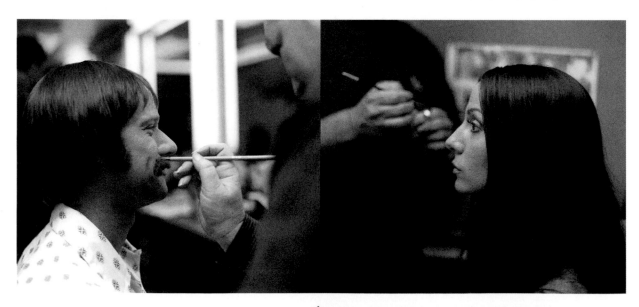

↑ BRUSH WITH FAME Jay Underwood and Renee Faia undergo some finishing touches before transforming into married '60s pop lovebirds Sonny and Cher for ABC's biopic, *And the Beat Goes On* (photographs by Deborah Schwartz)

↑ ALL'S *AFFAIR* IN LOVE AND WAR Ralph Fiennes and costar Julianne Moore got up close and personal for the making of Neil Jordan's wartime romance *The End of the Affair* (photograph by Isabel Snyder)

→ *MOON* LANDING After *The Truman Show*, Jim Carrey pointed his career toward drama again in '99. He stepped into the skin of late comedian Andy Kaufman for *Man on the Moon*, which chronicles the crazy life of the late *Taxi* star.

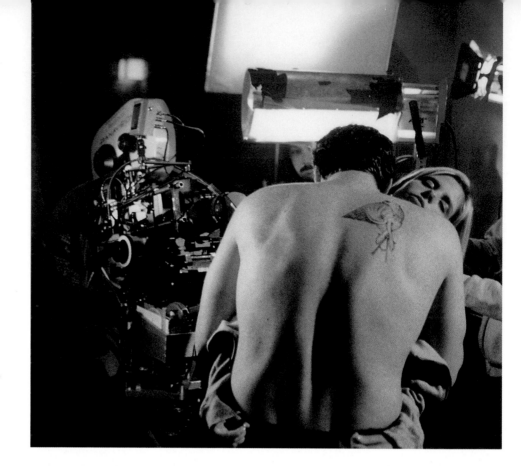

➡ GHOUL MEETS BOY Buffy, everyone's favorite teen stake wielder (Sarah Michelle Gellar), made the undead Angel's (David Boreanaz) blood boil on the set of The WB's *Buffy the Vampire Slayer*

⬇ SUSPENDER ANIMATION Tobey Maguire stars as John Irving's orphan hero Homer Wells in the film version of *The Cider House Rules*. On the set in New England, Maguire got a dab from a makeup artist (photograph by Mary Ellen Mark)

↑ GRAVEYARD SHIFT Johnny Depp's Ichabod Crane got ahead of himself while filming *Sleepy Hollow*. Director Tim Burton's retelling of the Headless Horseman legend was a fall hit (photograph by Mary Ellen Mark)

← FIT FOR A *KING* Jodie Foster had it made in the shade between takes of the costume drama *Anna and the King*, which costars Hong Kong action hero Chow Yun-Fat (photograph by Brigitte Lacombe)

↑ THE TALENTED MS. PALTROW Oscar winner Gwyneth paused for effect while making the psychological thriller *The Talented Mr. Ripley* (photograph by Brigitte Lacombe)

→ IT'S HIS SMALL WORLD Verne Troyer's Mini-Me in the *Austin Powers* sequel made audiences flip and made Troyer a fixture on the Hollywood scene (photograph by Moshe Brakha)

STYLE
BY DEGEN PENER

SARAH MICHELLE GELLAR

With a stunning turn at the Emmys, *Buffy the Vampire Slayer* star Sarah Michelle Gellar proved she could slay fashion critics as well as the undead. And she did it in a completely unorthodox color. "I had a dream that she was wearing turquoise," says Gellar's stylist, Jessica Paster. "She was like, 'I don't know about that.' I said, 'Trust me on this.'" Gellar, in a blue Grecian column by Vera Wang, updated the '60s minimalist look: Her hair (dyed honey blond just before the event) was pulled straight back. Her only accessory was an oversize turquoise beaded bracelet. "I felt more glamorous than ever that night," recalls Gellar, who stands out from the pack of other young Hollywood types by balancing elegance with a willingness to try new looks. So far, her youthful experimentation has paid off. To celebrate *Saturday Night Live*'s 25th anniversary (the show is six years older than she is), Gellar chose another color that can often overwhelm: bright orange. Her own beauty still shone through the shocking shade, though. Says Gellar: "I felt like a modern-day Cinderella."

A FASHION SLAYER Right, at the Emmys; above, from left: In Gucci; Buffy's got back at The WB's press tour; in Vera Wang for *SNL*'s 25th anniversary bash

CATHERINE ZETA-JONES

Her beauty is undeniable, highlighted by a stunning juxtaposition of raven hair and porcelain skin. But it's the way that Catherine Zeta-Jones moves—with a graceful, unforced sexiness—that makes her 1999's candidate for the Ava Gardner style hall of fame. The *Entrapment* star first wowed us at the Oscars in a fiery red Versace silk gown. "We redid the dress until it was perfect. It wasn't done until 11 p.m. the night before the show," recalls the actress' stylist, Fati Parsia, who adds, "I've never put her in red again. We've got to keep that special." Since then, Zeta-Jones, 30, has been turning up in a rainbow of other colors, from yellow to pink to soft lilac. "Catherine has a great sense of what she should look like," says Parsia. "When I met her, she was wearing a lot of black. I said, 'Catherine, we're going to go through a Van Gogh period.'" But while Zeta-Jones has been wearing more color—especially since her romance with Michael Douglas began—she's been wearing less jewelry. "There's been such an issue made of whether they are getting engaged that I've been using fewer and fewer rings," notes Parsia. "Every time she wore one it was like, 'Oh, she's getting married.'" Guess we'll just have to wait to see Zeta-Jones in white.

TREND-ZETA In a Thierry Mugler at Cannes; above, in a Christian Lacroix skirt and Gucci top; at the Oscars

CHARLIZE THERON

Even nonpareil vamps like Charlize Theron know when the price of looking fabulous runs too high. "There was this stunning Philip Treacy 'Jessica Rabbit' dress that I wore to the Fire & Ice Ball," says Theron, who herself was stunning in *The Devil's Advocate*, *Celebrity*, and 1999's *The Cider House Rules*. "It was fitted with a corset that shrunk my waist to nothing—but it came at the cost of being able to breathe. After a three-course meal, comfort over-rode vanity—I wore just my overcoat to the after-parties." That black dress, however, and a series of equally striking dark and slinky numbers that followed it turned Theron, 24, into one of the year's most starkly alluring visions. Because there's always an air of mystery when a blond wraps herself in the color of mid-night. "She's actually trying to stay away from black," says the actress' stylist, Cindy Evans. "But the dress she ends up liking the most, for one reason or another, is always the black one. But we do our best to seek out fashions that best capture her personality. It's sort of like dressing from the inside out—she's wildly vivacious, and she has a perfect balance of beauty and grace." And that's enough to take our breath away.

VA-VA-VAMP Right, at the Golden Globes in a beaded Halston; above left, the Treacy dress; in a Syren latex dress at the Oscars

ELIZABETH
HURLEY

What does a body like Elizabeth Hurley's deserve most? A little Las Vegas razzle-dazzle, a touch of Brit naughtiness, and some of the most sexy, revealing Versace gowns ever flaunted at a Hollywood party. "Versace suits her," says Hurley's stylist, Freddie Leiba. "They know how to cut dresses for a woman who's not a girlish model type. She has a womanly body." For almost every major event of 1999, Hurley, 34, wore an outfit by the designer and cast what has become her signature silhouette: a bosom-baring top, a leg-baring slit, and a tight, slinky line overall. Adds Leiba: "She's not self-conscious." The actress favors bright colors and galvanizing metallics that pack a punch. She also prefers staggeringly sharp stilettos by the likes of Jimmy Choo, Manolo Blahnik, and Gucci. But she keeps the rest of her look simple. Her slightly wavy hair rarely wavers in the way it's set, and she never wears earrings. Indeed, the only jewelry Hurley is ever spotted in is a diamond cross necklace that she wears everywhere. In fact, consistency seems to be Hurley's No. 1 style rule. "She knows exactly what works now," says Leiba. "It's not brain surgery." So what was Hurley's favorite style moment this year? The gown she wore to the London premiere of boyfriend Hugh Grant's *Mickey Blue Eyes*. "It was exquisitely cut," Hurley slyly recalls. "It made a very strange tinkling sound when I moved."

A HURLEY-GIG Left, at the *Mickey* premiere; above from left, slinky couture, skin-tight lavender, and shiny metallic, all by Versace

97

JENNIFER
LOPEZ

Here's a wardrobe challenge: How do you choose high-fashion looks to straddle not one but two successful careers? Check out Jennifer Lopez. For her role as a glamorous actress at the Oscars last spring, the *Out of Sight* star relied on a sumptuous Badgley Mischka gown in boldly contrasting black and white, and looked like a modern Grace Kelly. But for her new career as a singer promoting her debut album, *On the 6*, Lopez needed quite a different set of duds. Out went the ladylike dresses; in came a glam-but-casual style. "She was always very much this beautiful Hollywood starlet," says Lopez's stylist, Andrea Lieberman, "but we needed to separate the actress from the musician." In her pop-star guise, Lopez wore white halters, fringe tops, skimpy rhinestone dresses, and Gucci leather pants that played up both her sex appeal and her edge. "But we always balance it with something soft," adds Lieberman. "For instance, if she wears leather, she won't wear it in black but in a light color." But Lopez, 29, hasn't changed as much as you might think. Her new relaxed look gave her more opportunities to wear one of her favorite accessories: hoop earrings. Says Lieberman: "It's a style that's very Bronx, which is where she grew up."

OUTTA SIGHT Right, at the Oscars; above left, showing *6* sense in Gucci pants; in a halter by Versace

GWYNETH PALTROW

She's still the actress designers most want to dress. Gwyneth Paltrow, after becoming the darling of the fashion world in 1998, continued to live up to the 27-year-old's reputation as the most stylishly savvy girl in Hollywood. It began at the *Shakespeare in Love* premiere, where her ruler-straight 'do—instantly dubbed the Gwyneth look—helped kick off the major hair trend of the year. She continued to impress at the Golden Globes, giving instant popularity to another big look of the year, the full satin skirt. And it reached a peak at the Oscars, where she nabbed the Best Actress statuette in the most appropriate look a winner could wear: a total fantasyland pink Cinderella dress, courtesy of Ralph Lauren. And because Paltrow's poise and presence were so perfect, many fashion critics didn't even mind that the top of the dress had room to spare. As Old Navy's fashion lady Carrie Donovan told EW at the time: "The dress didn't even fit her that well, and she still looked great." Added E! Entertainment host Melissa Rivers: "She glows. It was like a pretty picture. And carrying an Oscar as an accessory isn't bad."

GWYN-WIN SITUATION Left, at the Oscars; the straight look (center); at the Globes in Calvin Klein

JULIA ROBERTS

It would be enough just to see Julia Roberts smile. But when that wonderful grin is set off by the actress' exquisite taste in clothes, the result is a vision of down-to-earth warmth and refined luxury. In '99, it was a pleasure to see that Roberts—once a poster girl for dressed-down, grungy thespians—had become one of the standard-bearers of Hollywood glamour. Her look isn't ostentatious (why gild this lily?), so Roberts, 32, sticks to dresses that are cut with the cleanest of lines. She often throws on an effortless-looking wrap. And one of her most prominent color choices this year, pink, was right in line with what was in vogue. But her favorite gown was a deceptively plain Calvin Klein that she wore to the New York premiere of *Notting Hill*: From the front it was a shapely column, yet when she turned around, it flirtatiously revealed an oval cutout in the back. "It was beautiful, comfortable, stylish, fabulous, and I love Calvin," says Roberts, who also wore one of the designer's gowns to the premiere of *Runaway Bride*, her other $100 million hit this year. The guy must bring her good luck. Says Klein: "Julia is one of those rare women who's got that look—natural, sexy, and elegant all at once—and it always seems easy, because it's intuitive."

RUNAWAY HIT Right, in Cynthia Rowley for a premiere above, Roberts in her Calvins—at *Bride*, left, and *Hill* debuts

RENE RUSSO

It's almost an insult to say that Rene Russo, 45, can look just as good as women half her age. That's because in 1999, Russo looked better and sexier—than the majority of actresses who crane for attention on the red carpet. Whether sparkling in an extremely revealing Halston dress in *The Thomas Crown Affair* or slinking through premieres in body-hugging gowns by her favorite designer, Celine, Russo is the height of refined stylishness. "Anybody who's ever known a great woman knows that we all ripen like fruit," says her stylist, Jane Ross. "The older you get, the better you get." Russo, whom Ross describes as "very non-fuss," is drawn to luxurious fabrics like cashmere. "She has an incredible eye for quality, a jeweler's eye," says Ross. "She loves beautiful things that are really well made." Also, the actress likes to keep her color scheme neutral—often either bold black or cool white—because of her auburn hair. And Ross adds that the silhouette you see in those formfitting gowns is always completely natural. "Those dresses take on the shape of her fantastic figure. When you've got a body like that, you don't need anybody else's line but your own." Good thing Russo isn't afraid to show it off. Recalls the star: "Kate Harrington [the costume designer for *Thomas Crown Affair*] walked in with something that looked like a handkerchief. She said, 'Rene, you don't have to wear it if you don't want to. Just try it on and see what you think.' I said, 'What? Where is it?' She opened her hand and I said, 'Why don't you just put sparkles on my body and be done with it?'"

AFFAIR LADY Russo relies on Celine: left, in an elegant beaded gown; above from left, casual crystal jeans; an all-leather look; shimmering in white

KERI RUSSELL

It's easy for young stars, completely new to the celebrity fashion sweepstakes, to mess up big time. Some try to be too trendy, wearing the overdone fads of the moment. Others are so conservative they look far older than their years. More than anyone, Keri Russell, 23, better known as TV's Felicity, stood out by striking a balance between sophisticated glamour and youthful ease in her major appearances this year. And she did it by making a smart choice: gowns by Giorgio Armani. "The Golden Globes was my first real dress-up event," says the actress, who was deluged by different designers. Armani won her over by sending her a two-piece outfit, in fearless orange, that got her look just right. "It was formal and yet something I thought was still cool," recalls Russell. Says the designer, "What I like about Keri is her elegant style and her understated sense of fashion. All things close to my heart." Russell decided to pair the dress with something other than vertiginous high heels. "I got to wear flip-flops," she laughs. So when the Emmys rolled around, Russell knew whom to go back to. For the ceremony, which is an even bigger dress-up event, she chose another Armani, a light blue column with a lavender wrap that was the peak of uncontrived elegance. But were there flip-flops under there? Unlikely, but Russell isn't saying.

OH, GIORGIO! Right, in Armani for the Emmys and, above left, the Globes. Casual in Dolce & Gabbana at the MTV Movie Awards.

TLC

These days, we look back at the '70s-era Cher as a paragon who defined her decade. The same thing might just happen to the three women of the best-selling pop-hop group TLC. Their '90s look—inspired by the cyberspace revolution—walks a fine line between rock-star cool and just plain bizarre. But love it or hate it, it's never boring. "Their clothes [this year] go with the theme of their album, *FanMail*, which is about the future and all things virtual," says TLC stylist and designer Julie Mijares. In September, the threesome—Tionne "T-Boz" Watkins, 29, Lisa "Left Eye" Lopes, 28, and Rozonda "Chilli" Thomas, 29—created a sci-fi spectacle at the *MTV Video Music Awards* in black leather outfits with tiny mirrors sewn into them. In the video for their hit single "No Scrubs," they wore black ensembles in high-tech materials like neoprene and vinyl that were accessorized with rave-style flashing lights. (They wore red versions at the MTV awards.) And for their "Unpretty" video, they went techno-transcendental in what Mijares describes as "futuristic Balinese costumes worn with belly chains. Most of the time their clothes are custom-made." In fact, TLC has a hard time wearing many designer ensembles. "The [women] are so tiny," says Mijares, "it's hard to find anything in the showrooms that fit them. They are like little munchkins with these incredible bodies. The tallest is 5 foot 1." You'd never know it from the meteor-size splash they've made.

TAKE THREE Top, reason for reflection at MTV's Video Music Awards. Above, Left Eye gets foxy in a Kyle Young skirt; their sparkling MTV performance in red lighted outfits.

It's all about expectations—exceeding them, that is. And as the millennium drew to a close, EW's critics waded through knee-high wheat and waist-high chaff to select the best offerings of 1999, a year we once associated with flying cars, robotic servants, and lightsabers. In retrospect, those futuristic mainstays look quaint, especially compared with what actually transpired. Jedi Knights and rapping cowboys left audiences cold, but a low-tech thriller became an overnight smash. A famous comic blurred the line between fantasy and reality by *inhabiting* the role of...a famous comic who blurred the line between fantasy and reality. And some nut dropped a camera inside John Malkovich's head. Predictability went out of fashion.

BEST
+
WORST

On TV, mobsters got analyzed, geeks got freaky, and John Goodman got a svelte new bod—without assistance from a laugh track. Meanwhile, songstress Fiona Apple emerged from the din of teen pop and smashed the sophomore-slump stigma to smithereens. And one manic boy-band refugee demonstrated the appeal of a huge *Ego*. We expected bigger and better. We got shorter and sweeter. Story collections proved more sublime than some high-profile novels; downloadable music made CDs unwieldy by comparison. And what of the droids and lightsabers? Well, there's always AIBO the robo-dog—a winner in any paradigm and a comfort to all of you old-fashioned futurists. Buck up, fellows. You've got a thousand more years to get that flying car off the ground.

1

MAN ON THE MOON

Comedian, mass-media joker, walking personality crisis: Andy Kaufman was all of these things, and the joy of *Man on the Moon* is the way that screenwriters Scott Alexander and Larry Karaszewski and director Milos Forman transform Kaufman's dance of life and performance into a dizzying and maniacally funny celebration of American showbiz. Jim Carrey's eerie, virtuosic impersonation doesn't tell us who Kaufman was inside exactly, yet it captures the delirious thrill he took in making every moment a charade, perpetually playing someone else in order to play with your head. He was Latka Gravas and Elvis Presley, wanton woman-wrestler and man on the moon—a sweet, spectral nerd forever split off from his scabrous, lounge-demon id, Tony Clifton. With a couple of decades' hindsight, the movie reassembles Kaufman into a cracked prophet of the Entertainment Age, a wild-man prankster who created his own form of hocus-pocus guerrilla theater. The teasing upshot is that only someone who was *this* disconnected, this much of a stranger even to himself, could have gone to such fearless and demented lengths to connect with an audience. In its celebration of Andy Kaufman's obsessive desire to burst the fourth wall, to leave you laughing with your jaw on the floor, *Man on the Moon*, more than *The Truman Show* or *Being John Malkovich*, emerges as a great, exhilarating fable for the era of virtual identity.

2 TOPSY-TURVY Miraculously, Mike Leigh's merry, haunting, ebullient epic about Gilbert and Sullivan seems to wipe away every period piece you've seen. It's as if you'd climbed into a time machine and landed in the hidden heart of Victorian London, a world of civilized high spirits in which the courtliness of even the most trivial encounter becomes at once delectable and deeply enigmatic—a playful cover for the sensuality beneath. (Here, it's mind and body that are topsy-turvy.) The film understands that William S. Gilbert (Jim Broadbent), the dour clockwork lyricist trapped in his mathematical absurdism, and Sir Arthur Sullivan (Allan Corduner), the blissed-out composer-conductor imp, weren't creating high art. But as it follows a crucial moment late in their careers, when the famous duo part ways, reunite, and then—in what may be the most intimate and rapturous backstage theater chronicle ever filmed—create and stage *The Mikado*, the movie becomes a transcendent celebration of the English soul, of a lost empire founded on the beauty of order.

3 BOYS DON'T CRY What made Teena Brandon, a wayward loner drifting through rural Nebraska in the early '90s, want to pass herself off as a rough-and-tumble young man named Brandon Teena? The answer is assuredly "psychosexual," but the galvanizing power of Kimberly Peirce's starkly lyrical first feature is that it dramatizes this daredev-

MAN ON THE MOON

il role reversal in the American badlands as a blind quest for freedom—as the story of a girl driven to own a boy's experience in a man's world. The extraordinary Hilary Swank plays Brandon as a complex series of juggled personalities, yet beneath that, her fragile yearnings are naked and raw. *Boys Don't Cry* has some of the plainsong intensity and shock of Norman Mailer's *The Executioner's Song*, especially in its violent and devastating final chapter, when the movie descends into the blackness of tabloid tragedy.

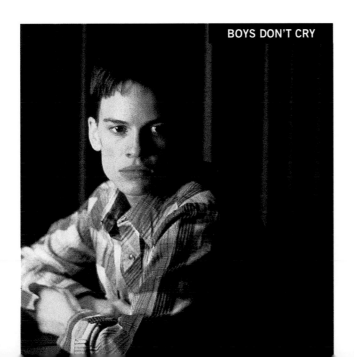

BOYS DON'T CRY

4 RUN LOLA RUN It moves with the zigzag velocity of an MTV fever dream and "resets" itself like a cinematic Nintendo game, but Tom Tykwer's bedazzling tale of love, karma, and a flame-haired Berlin punkette named Lola is much more than a pulsating flash machine. In the razor-cut precision with which it spins out three intricately different versions of Lola's pavement-pounding odyssey, the movie is really an examination of what it takes to change a moment, and with it the world. In one heady humane rush, Tykwer brings European cinema whooshing into the next century, leaving you thrilled, dazed, and—always—breathless.

5 MR. DEATH: THE RISE AND FALL OF FRED A. LEUCHTER, JR. The first truly great film from documentarian Errol Morris plugs you into the avuncular and very, very scary mind of a singular American oddball: Fred Leuchter, a nebbishy designer of better capital-punishment machines who is recruited by an infamous Holocaust denier to make a "scientific" study debunking the gas chambers at Auschwitz. Fred prides himself on drinking 40 cups of coffee a day; he's alert but blind. As we watch him in the death camp, scraping away to collect his samples yet blithely oblivious to the ghosts around him, the movie becomes an extraordinary sick-joke parable of 20th-century bureaucratic indifference. Morris' gaze is as cold and acerbic as ever, but at long last he has found a subject that's worthy of it.

6 GO The thrill of a joyride is that it lets you tune out everything but the moment. Doug Liman's time-twisting, rave-generation ensemble bash, a kind of junior *Pulp Fiction* sprinkled with the sweet middle-class romanticism of *American Graffiti*, sends a dozen young L.A. wanderers out into the night. We're invited to share their compulsive

ELECTION

search for kicks, yet the movie also homes in on the real-world intimacy of each moment, in all its danger and sexy promise and throwaway grace. Liman, fresh from *Swingers*, once again reclaims Las Vegas as a camp paradise for post-boomers—a place to try on a fake persona like a new suit of clothes—and he proves a true wizard with actors. From Sarah Polley to Taye Diggs to Timothy Olyphant, the cast of *Go* is a talent-drenched brat pack for the next millennium.

7 BEING JOHN MALKOVICH Great surrealists have always understood that the most profoundly warped worlds are just a fun-house-mirror bend away from ours. In his ticklish, perception-skewering first feature, director Spike Jonze ushers you into a casually Kafkaesque office space through which the characters can literally enter the mind of John Malkovich; once in his head, they're never more themselves. Why Malkovich? Because he's nearly invisible in his own celebrity. He needs his occupiers as much as they need him. Jonze risks overdosing on dream logic (if only one could say that for other filmmakers!), but then, the imagination run amok is his subject as well as his style. To be a movie star, a dangling puppet, a woman making love through a man's body—everyone in *Being John Malkovich* fervently wants to be someone else, and once they pass through the portal of personality, the movie feels no weirder, or less inviting, than a trip to Wonderland or Oz.

DOGMA

8 ELECTION In a year of doublespeak political candidates and hyped-up fight clubs, Alexander Payne's delicious satirical drama delivered the most pungent portrait yet of the deflated modern male. In this case, he's a sexually desperate, too-nice-for-his-own-good high school teacher (Matthew Broderick) who acts out his horny frustration by trying to trip up the rabid student overachiever running for class president. The praise for Reese Witherspoon's fanatical feistiness overshadowed Broderick's exquisitely bold and funny performance as a benevolent sap-turned-scoundrel. *Election*, which is like *American Beauty* minus the bombast, marks Payne as a fearless chronicler of suburban hypocrisy and desire. It tells the real story of American success: who gets it, who doesn't, and why.

9 THE BLAIR WITCH PROJECT How is it that a grainy, clever, lost-in-the-woods horror movie, shot with handheld video cameras that made the whole thing look like a satanic episode of *Road Rules*, ended up not just the most talked-about but—to many—the most reviled movie of the year? The people who complained that it simply "wasn't scary" seemed to be evaluating it on some hardened consumer shock meter: *Either I leap out of my seat in terror or it sucks!* Well, *Blair Witch* didn't make me leap out of my seat. It did, however, draw me into that childish dread of the dark—not Hollywood-thriller dark, but genuine, godforsaken *night*. The drama of the movie lies in how its glib, squabbling characters, all professional twentysomething ironists, receive their comeuppance. They've been taking in life through video, a secular medium that won't allow for mystery, but, like the viewer, they believe by the end that maybe, in that dingy blackened midnight house, there is something you don't want to see, that you have to see, and keep looking for....

10 DOGMA Its only sin is its cinematography. It took a professional rascal like Kevin Smith, who writes naughty jokes with evangelical fervor, to make a heavenly religious movie rooted in the imperfections of earth. The tale of two bad-boy angels who try to win their way back into God's good graces, *Dogma* is as scrappy (and funny) as an underground comic book, yet it so believes in everything it's showing you—a world of celestial beings hooked on Catholic debate—that it makes you a believer, too.

THE WORST

DOUBLE JEOPARDY A don't-get-mad-get-even thriller of such staggering idiocy and contrivance that its vengeance seems to be directed mostly against the art of storytelling. As a woman who is wrongly convicted of killing her husband, and can therefore now kill him for real (yeah, right), Ashley Judd steers a car while handcuffed to the door, yet she can't think to phone an attorney in jail. It's about time a movie proved that women's taste can be as awful as men's.

BEING JOHN MALKOVICH

1

THE SOPRANOS

(HBO) It's all but certain that no other show in the history of TV critics' 10-best lists will appear at the top of more of 'em than this one. *The Sopranos* is the *Sgt. Pepper's Lonely Hearts Club Band* of television, the first epic-scale work in the medium about whose impact and originality everyone can agree. Ignoring notions of conventional TV heroes, and yoking together two of the late 20th century's most influential phenomena—psychiatric therapy and *The Godfather* (Puzo sourcebook and Coppola movies)—creator David Chase not only pulled off the year's most emotionally complex and gut-level-entertaining series but brought forth a drama that provoked fervent discussion among a wide, avid audience. No matter what the quality of the next batch of episodes premiering in January is, the richness of these first 13 will endure in a way most programming never even attempts.

2

BUFFY THE VAMPIRE SLAYER *(The WB)* and **ANGEL** *(The WB)* Like a shrewd blackjack player, writer-producer Joss Whedon doubled-down this season, splitting Buffy Summers from her love interest by sending the broad-shouldered vampire Angel to fight evil in Los Angeles. The result? A familiar show stepping into fresh territory: college life (and an underground rebel group as interested in vampires and demons as the Slayer is), plus a spin-off full of swirling film-noir promise.

BUFFY THE VAMPIRE SLAYER

THE SOPRANOS

3 FREAKS AND GEEKS *(NBC)* The year's most pleasant surprise: an hour-long, '80s-themed comedy about the misery of adolescence that is as unexpectedly open to small, delicate emotions as it is to big belly laughs. Featuring the season's finest ensemble of young actors, *Freaks* possesses all the qualities that the touted young-adult bomb *Wasteland* wanted to have but could only fake: warmth, truth, sincerity. And when was the last time that trio provided the basis for wild humor?

4 ONCE AND AGAIN *(ABC)* Already pegged a loser because the soggy *Judging Amy* beats it in the ratings, this tale of a divorced dad (Billy Campbell) and separated mom (Sela Ward) discomfits those people who've found producers Marshall Herskovitz and Ed Zwick's previous shows, *thirtysomething* and *My So-Called Life*, equally squirmy—folks who don't like to admit how self-absorbed we tend to be, and how, with good intentions and hard work, self-absorption can be transmuted into (in the case of life) selfless devotion and (in the case of TV) sterling drama.

5 NOW AND AGAIN *(CBS)* As the brains behind the year's most surprising romance/comedy/sci-fi drama, Glenn Gordon Caron has obviously learned a few things from his long TV absence since *Moonlighting*—foremost among them: Don't just rely on your two main stars. Margaret Colin and Eric Close are marvy,

but so is Dennis Haysbert as Close's impishly imperious boss, and so is Gerrit Graham as a perennially confused family friend, and so is Heather Matarazzo as their sweet, all-accepting daughter. All this, plus strong ratings in the ghetto of Fridays at 9—the wonders of network television never cease.

NOW AND AGAIN

FREAKS AND GEEKS

6 THE WEST WING *(NBC)* and SPORTS NIGHT *(ABC)* One is an hour drama, the other a 30-minute dramedy; both are created and (most nights) written by Aaron Sorkin. Each seems to contain twice the amount of dialogue their genres usually demand, yet the talk has a purpose: It's Sorkin's heightened-reality way of conveying the tension and exhausting pace of the workplace, and who can't relate to that? Sure, *Wing*'s labor site is the White House (with a revved-up Martin Sheen as a wily, intellectually adept but instinct-driven President any political party should wish it had) and *Sports Night*'s is a TV studio, but that doesn't detract from the universality of backbiting, misunderstandings, and power grabs. These shows are two good arguments against the notion that TV is best when it's mere escapism.

7 THE X-FILES *(Fox)* Still crazy after all these years. Creator Chris Carter's dilemma—and our ongoing pleasure—is that the more he makes clear that he's always known where all the mayhem, mysticism, and sci-fi are heading, the less we care. For most of us, the trip—the relationship between Mulder and Scully (capped by a tender millennium kiss), or the rare corker of a stand-alone script, like the one Vince Gilligan penned about a guy who could peel off his ears and eat your brain—is its own reward.

8 FRIENDS *(NBC)* The airiest of all the enduring sitcoms just keeps floating along on its own comic high with this season's plot-propelling notion—that wisecracking, stuttery Chandler Bing (Matthew Perry) and picky, earnest Monica Geller (Courteney Cox Arquette) just may last as an odd-couple couple—playing out with deeply satisfying laughs. Best supporting player this year: Matt LeBlanc's Joey, miraculously finding new ways to be lovably stupid, week after week. The guy deserves an Emmy.

THE WEST WING

THE SIMPSONS

TV'S TOP 10 REGULAR SERIES		AVG. VIEWERSHIP*
1.	ER (NBC)	20.0
2.	NFL MONDAY NIGHT FOOTBALL (ABC)	19.5
3.	FRIENDS (NBC)	18.8
4.	FRASIER (NBC)	18.4
5.	TOUCHED BY AN ANGEL (CBS)	16.4
	STARK RAVING MAD (NBC)	16.4
	60 MINUTES (CBS)	16.4
8.	JUDGING AMY (CBS)	15.4
9.	EVERYBODY LOVES RAYMOND (CBS)	14.9
10.	JESSE (NBC)	14.7

*IN MILLIONS; SOURCE: NIELSEN MEDIA RESEARCH; THROUGH DECEMBER 5, 1999

not only bowled but sang the first version of the Doors' "The End" that I've ever found bearable, can stand with any in the series' decade-long history.

10 FELICITY *(The WB)* Her hair may be short, but Felicity (Keri Russell) is long on heart, soul, and humor—Russell is, in fact, underrated as a deadpan comedian in her reactions to all her oddball student friends and her two primary handsome fellas, Ben (Scott Speedman) and Noel (Scott Foley). How refreshing that, as I write, she's not involved with either of them—she may look waifish, but she's an independent gal in what is easily the best-written large-ensemble young-adult show on TV.

THE BEST TV SHOW YOU'LL PROBABLY NEVER SEE
QUEER AS FOLK Had any U.S. network had the guts to air it, *Queer as Folk* would be at No. 2 on my top 10 list. But the fact that this ribald, witty, unexpectedly moving British miniseries featured, in its first hour, a rakish antihero (the roguishly beguiling Aidan Gillen) having sex with a 15-year-old boy was enough to consign it to gay film festivals and bootlegged Internet video sales over here. Created by Russell T. Davies, *Folk* is a tale of gay men's lives in all their complexity—sex being just one aspect that's explored. Joel Schumacher is planning a version for Showtime with the youngest character upped to legal age, but excuse me if I doubt that anyone could ever improve upon the original.

9 THE SIMPSONS *(Fox)* And the laughs just keep on coming: TV's longest-running cartoon sustains itself by clinging to the idea of family as lifeline—in this sense, it's the opposite of the artful navel-gazing of *Once and Again* and, despite its format, every bit as realistic. *The Simpsons* explores fears about getting expelled, getting fired, getting fat, and getting drunk, as well as celebrating the occasional triumph, like rolling a perfect 300 in bowling. Indeed, the Nov. 14 episode, in which Homer

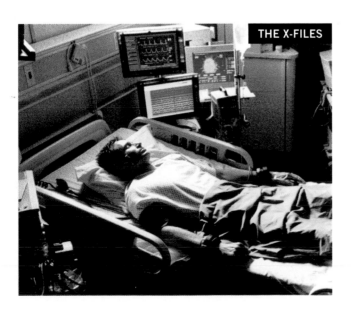

THE X-FILES

THE WORST

FAMILY GUY *(Fox)* It has racist, anti-Semitic, and AIDS jokes; shoddy animation; and stolen ideas. The cartoon as vile swill.

TOP 10
MUSIC

BY DAVID BROWNE

WILLIAMS

① 1

THE EGO HAS LANDED

ROBBIE WILLIAMS *(Capitol)* Unless you count (a) the ascent of straight-outta-fraternities white rappers or (b) the augmentation of breasts, 1999 wasn't much of a year for innovation or breakthroughs. Precious little stood up and announced itself the way Nirvana, Dr. Dre, or Lauryn Hill, to name just a few, did in the past decade. Instead, we had to settle for craft and record-making skills, and in that respect, the past year was a pretty sensational one. Choose Shania or Ricky if you must, but in the realm of pop entertainment, I'll opt for this British bad boy, whose debut American album (cobbled together from two British releases) is an all-you-can-hum smorgasbord. From Euro-pop truffles ("Millennium," "No Regrets") to rueful pub rock ("Win Some Lose Some," "Old Before I Die") to stadium-friendly ballads ("Angels," "Strong") that would have easily fit onto old, pre-schlock Elton John albums, *The Ego Has Landed* takes a broad, internationalist view of pop. Starting with its title, it's hard to recall a more roguishly appealing record this year. And unlike most of his competition for Top 40 radio play, Williams has a genuine rough-edged personality—a last-call-of-the-night feistiness revealed in his hard-bloke's-night delivery, unrepentant-layabout lyrics (including one of the year's smartest couplets: "Every morning when I wake up/I look like Kiss but without the makeup"), and stage persona, which can best be described as a laddie-culture version of James Bond. Williams' pop rivals may have outsold him in the colonies, but no matter; he's a true backstreet boy.

2 WHEN THE PAWN... / FIONA APPLE (*Clean Slate/Epic*) Guffaw if you will at the audacity of a 90-word album title (sorry, readers, but I'm not squandering another 87 here), but there's nothing laughable about this quantum leap in Apple's talent. On her second album, the gawky teen waif of 1996 becomes a psychologically embattled chanteuse of 22, self-absorbedly picking over her mental foibles and those of her lover (*Boogie Nights* director Paul Thomas Anderson). Whatever the subject of her songs, Apple is constantly torn between fire-breathing anger and lacerating self-criticism; the album could have been called *She Loves Me, She Loves Me Nuts*. Yet her gift for melodically gothic songs, her sensually throaty voice, and the snaky, playfully screwy arrangements of producer Jon Brion keep Apple more than on track. *When the Pawn...* is spellbinding supper-club music for the post-Prozac generation. It doesn't merely beat the second-album jinx but stares it down with scrutinizing, bugged-out eyes. While many of her Lilith Fair peers wilted on the cultural vine in '99, Apple emerged as an artist of emotional and musical complexity. She's nobody's pawn.

APPLE

MOBY

3 "I WANT IT THAT WAY" / BACKSTREET BOYS (*Jive, single*) Their *Millennium* album had such a surfeit of smarmy ooze that its running time felt like a thousand years, but this glistening single was a marvel of seamless song craft and studio polish. And unlike "Livin' La Vida Loca," it sounded better every time it aired on the radio (which was, needless to say, continuously). That hook of a chorus, that amusingly ambiguous refrain (you want it which way?), those intertwining vocal gulps and sighs—finally, here was something that made the all-consuming wimpiness of the boy-band brigade seem noble. The last great pop single of the actual millennium, "I Want It That Way" compensated for a year's worth of BSB and Britney Spears clones. Well, almost.

4 PLAY / MOBY (*V2*) Had it been first released this year instead of late in '98, Fatboy Slim's spirit-lifting "Praise You" (and its brilliantly warped, Spike Jonze–directed video) would be on this list. Instead, the slot is awarded to Moby's continually beguiling album, which expands upon the same recontextualizing concept as Fatboy's single. In lifting old blues and gospel chants, field hollers, and old-school raps from their original surroundings and setting them down on beds of clubland pulses and post-blaxploitation grooves, Moby risked making a patronizing novelty album. But the results are just the opposite—*Play* is music of radiance, power, and grit. At a time when sampling has replaced the guitar solo as de rigueur on records, the ghosts in these machines never sounded so inspirational.

BACKSTREET BOYS

5 "NO SCRUBS" / TLC *(LaFace/Arista, single)* Before they started taking swipes at each other, these dysfunctional divas took unified aim at the hangers-on and hitters-on in their lives. In a year in which pop women (from Shania and the Dixie Chicks to Eve, and even Christina Aguilera) strutted their assertiveness and pliant males (Marc Anthony, Tal Bachman, the somewhat reformed Anthony Kiedis of the Red Hot Chili Peppers) were happy to let them, "No Scrubs" was very much a zeitgeist moment, inserting

new slang into the national vocabulary and even inspiring an answer record (Sporty Thievz's "No Pigeons"). Thanks to producer and cowriter Kevin Briggs, it was also a smooth, silky hang glider of a single. "Unpretty," the Top 40 follow-up from TLC's otherwise spotty *FanMail* album, was a worthy successor.

6 BEAUCOUP FISH / UNDERWORLD *(JBO/V2)* Cynics can scoff at the so-called electronica revolution of several years back, but anyone who dismisses this British trio's addictive third album deserves to be saddled with the sadly eviscerated remains of alternative rock. (Solving every Y2K computer glitch must be a less laborious process than plowing through both discs of Nine Inch Nails' *The Fragile*.) Like the fish of its title, *Beaucoup* makes you feel as if you're drifting pleasurably in an undercurrent of sound. And not merely the usual techno whirs and bleeps: Seamlessly blending hooks, balladry, and vocalist Karl Hyde's seductive growl into its pulsating-heartbeat soundscapes, the album is ambient but perpetually grounded. It also stirs up a machine-clanging racket when it wants to. Underworld more than fulfill the promise of their "Born Slippy" single (from *Trainspotting*); they search for an even braver new-music world and find it.

7 "LADYFINGERS" / LUSCIOUS JACKSON *(Grand Royal/ Capitol, single)* This is the delicious cream puff they've always had in them, bringing together their rap-singing style, hip-swaying sense of melody, and girl-group harmonies straight from the urban jungle. With Emmylou

LUSCIOUS JACKSON

ORTON

Harris adding a few luscious *oohs* and *aahs* of her own, lead singer and guitarist Jill Cunniff drops her armor just enough to flash a few displays of heart—while still reminding the object of her affection that a suitcase is standing by just in case he makes any wrong moves. Post-smirking sincerity from the Beastie Boys' Grand Royal label; if that's not a sign of the times, nothing is. (Other notable summertime radio treats: Len's "Steal My Sunshine," Basement Jaxx's "Red Alert," and Madonna's "Beautiful Stranger.")

8 CENTRAL RESERVATION / BETH ORTON *(Arista)* With her drawn-shades voice and penchant for doleful observations, British folkie Orton is the definition of an oldfangled, introspective, fatalistic coffeehouse troubadour. She's such a rarity, especially in the world of record-company conglomerates, that you half expect to find her in a Rock and Roll Hall of Fame exhibit of extinct species. Orton's second album, though, is the farthest thing from musty. *Central Reservation*'s shifting array of backdrops—lightly flickering techno, pop-standards orchestration, jazzy cabaret, sinuous rock—caress and perk up these regret-laden songs and Orton's delivery. The year's most resplendently sad music.

THE WORST

ON THE 6 / JENNIFER LOPEZ *(Work Group)* How sad that so much of this year's Latin-music boom had so little to do with Latin music. Ricky Martin's and Marc Anthony's Anglo crossovers felt as tasteless as Latino fast food—El Happy Meals. The genre's dynamism and crackling energy were ground into crossover pulp. But what was worse: squandering Anthony's voice or spending millions attempting to transform actress Lopez into a cut-rate Gloria Estefan? This appallingly pallid set of vanilla ballads, limp rap, and diluted fiesta pop was an insult not just to Latin music but to music in general. Nice album cover, though.

9 BLACK ON BOTH SIDES / MOS DEF *(Rawkus)* Kool Keith was wickedly funnier and the suddenly under-rated Missy "Misdemeanor" Elliott more sonically ambitious. Yet by year's end, the New York rapper's first solo album (following this year's promising Black Star group project) was 1999's most pleasurable and continually enjoyable hip-hop record. Whether espousing neighborhood and racial pride or rhyming about discrimination, ecology, and the precise U.S. defense budget (and how it compared with poverty statistics!), Mos Def is never less than serious-minded. His secret weapon is his music. Keeping it light but never lightweight, he breaks into singsong raps, quotes the Chili Peppers' "Under the Bridge," imitates reggae star Gregory Isaacs, and swaddles his rhymes in jazz organ, punk-funk, and soul horn sections. Like a modern-day Muhammad Ali, Mos Def floats like a hip-hop butterfly, but stings like a Brooklyn bee.

10 THE THREE EP'S / THE BETA BAND *(Astralwerks)* These enigmatic Scottish noisemakers released two albums over the past year, with this compilation of U.K. EPs slightly better than the subsequent *The Beta Band*. In contrast to more orthodox folkie rockers, the Betas' concept of roots music is a mutant mixture. They're given to strum-in-cheek mantras with shaken-cereal-box rhythms and languid grooves—it's as if Beck and John Cage visited the Moody Blues' retirement villa and jammed all night long. Even when their experiments go a tad awry, they're always worth hearing. Just as important, the Beta Band remember a time when rock was a thing of mystery and allure, rather than coiled-up tantrums.

1

CLOSE RANGE

Annie Proulx *(Scribner, $25)* It was a renaissance year for short stories, as readers and publishers alike once again embraced the abbreviated form. From Gish Jen's *Who's Irish?* to Jhumpa Lahiri's *Interpreter of Maladies*, short-story collections thrived in both content and sales—and for the first time, one of them has been selected as EW's best book of the year. Annie Proulx's masterful collection *Close Range*, a gorgeously nuanced series of tales set in Wyoming's stark ranchland, shows just how rich a subject ordinary lives can be. In "Job History," one man's blue-collar existence is condensed into a seemingly dispassionate list of events; "The Mud Below" tells the melancholy tale of a wandering rodeo rider; a foolish old man on a doomed journey to his brother's funeral is the subject of "A Half-Skinned Steer." From cowboys to drug addicts, Proulx creates palpably real, familiar characters, and offers a stunning portrait of a bleak Western world.

2 **AMY AND ISABELLE** Elizabeth Strout *(Random House, $22.95)* The mother-daughter bond has always been juicy fodder for literature. Unfortunately, because it's been done so many times, it's easy to overlook gems like Strout's. But don't: *Amy and Isabelle* is a truly shimmering debut about a teenage girl, her repressed mother, and the secrets that keep them apart.

3 **WAITING** Ha Jin *(Pantheon, $24)* The 1999 National Book Award winner for fiction explores the natures of desire and traditional family duty through the eyes of a Chinese doctor torn between his girlfriend and his village wife, whom he has been attempting to divorce for 17 years. Jin's prose is graceful throughout, but it's the story's elegantly ironic denouement that makes *Waiting* such a satisfying depiction of human yearning.

4 **FOR THE RELIEF OF UNBEARABLE URGES** Nathan Englander *(Knopf, $22)* A homely woman caught in a suffocating arranged marriage. A frustrated husband who receives a rabbi's dispensation to visit a prostitute—and gets VD. A Brooklyn wigmaker who pines for her bygone youth. No matter the premise, Englander's nine stunningly crafted stories illuminate not just a specific community of Orthodox Jews, but universal relationships and desires.

5 **A STAR CALLED HENRY** Roddy Doyle *(Viking, $24.95)* Henry Smart is a street urchin–turned–IRA assassin who uses his father's wooden leg as a talisman and never wants for conquests. What elevates this rakish character beyond mere hero-boy status is that he's the star of an utterly heartrending historical account of the brutal struggle for Irish independence. The first book in a projected trilogy, *A Star Called Henry* is painted with the same gutsy, visceral prose that made Doyle's *The Commitments* and *Paddy Clarke Ha Ha Ha* such canny delights.

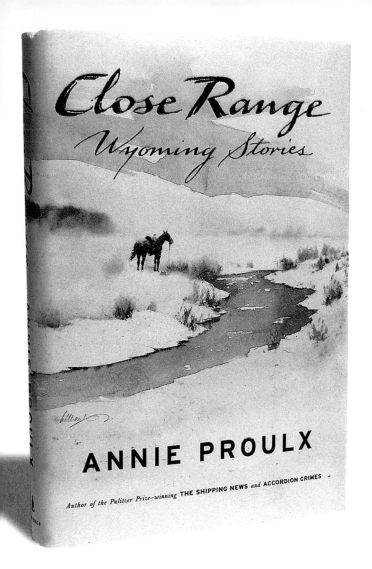

CLOSE RANGE: Wyoming Stories
ANNIE PROULX
Author of the Pulitzer Prize–winning THE SHIPPING NEWS and ACCORDION CRIMES

Barbara Havers, to figure out what went down. In her latest thoroughly British thriller (book 10 of the wildly popular series), American author George serves up a smashing mix of pitch-perfect Brit dialogue, a meticulously researched sense of place, and impeccably drawn characters. Some may call it too graphic and—clocking in at 594 pages—too long. We call it bloody marvelous.

8 CRUDDY Lynda Barry *(Simon & Schuster, $23)* The cartoonist proves she can write beyond comic-strip confines in this hilariously macabre novel. Framed as a suicide note written by a teenager named Roberta, *Cruddy* interweaves two narratives: one of Roberta at 11, the other of her five years later. The drug-hazed tale is all the more impressive because it depicts the horror of a mangled family without a shred of self-pity.

9 HEADLONG Michael Frayn *(Metropolitan Books, $26)* "Many of the world's great treasures are known to be lost...I believe I may have found one of them." Thus begins the deliciously tragicomic story of Martin Clay, a philosopher who's convinced he's discovered a long-lost Brueghel. In witty, wicked prose, Frayn details the lengths Clay will go to obtain the painting—and offers a gleefully sharp picture of irrational obsession.

10 DUTCH: A MEMOIR OF RONALD REAGAN Edmund Morris *(Random House, $35)* With all the ruckus surrounding Reagan biographer Morris' conceit—inserting himself into the narrative as a fictional character who interacts with the former President—we're all forgetting that truth is relative. Especially when it's as gracefully written and imaginative as this. With its believable, re-created dialogue and lovely descriptions of what could (conceivably) have been, the 14-years-in-the-making *Dutch* is surely one of the most thoroughly researched novels ever.

6 PERSONAL INJURIES Scott Turow *(Farrar, Straus & Giroux, $27)* Unlike some of his legal-thriller contemporaries, Turow isn't about to be rushed into cranking out a gazillion-selling yarn every year. Lucky for us. This story of oily yet likable attorney Robbie Feaver (and the FBI sting that hinges on his cooperation)—is an expertly crafted, colorfully peopled tale. And it's also a gazillion-seller.

7 IN PURSUIT OF THE PROPER SINNER Elizabeth George *(Bantam, $25.95)* Two grisly murders were committed in the remote Derbyshire moors, and it's up to Det. Thomas Lynley and his recently disgraced partner,

THE WORST

NICHOLAS SPARKS
A Walk to Remember

A WALK TO REMEMBER **Nicholas Sparks** *(Warner, $19.95)* Boy meets girl. Boy falls in love. Boy and girl become orphanage-visiting do-gooders. Girl has secret. Boy evolves. Novel reads like a bad *Afterschool Special*. From the author of *Message in a Bottle.*

ENGLANDER

THE WIZARD OF OZ DVD

(Warner, G) As the calendar flips over into a new millennium—and the clock on your VCR still blinks "12:00"—it is no longer possible to ignore the DVD revolution. Simply put, *this* is how we should be watching movies at home. Two 1999 discs make it a case-closed situation, and since naming one of them *the* best would require the services of a Solomon, I'll just choose the movie with which I have the more personal relationship. Which is to say that seeing *The Wizard of Oz* on DVD made me feel 7 years old again. That was the year my father bought a color TV set, and Dorothy's opening of the door onto a riot of Technicolor hit my tiny brain like a Froot Loops high, only better. I felt the same sensation—compounded by nostalgia—when I beheld the same scene this year on DVD and marveled at the details that smeary old VHS tapes had hidden, up to and including every brick in the Yellow Brick Road. It was as if my memory itself had been squeegeed clean. Here's some of what else you get on the *Wizard* disc: a making-of documentary; trailers, posters, sketches, and storyboards; makeup and costume tests; studio publicity stills and memos; home-movie footage of the deleted "Jitterbug" dance sequence; clips from a 1914 version of *Oz* written and directed by L. Frank Baum; 1979 interviews with Margaret Hamilton, Jack Haley, and Ray Bolger; *and* hours of audio-only musical takes, including Judy Garland's first public performance of "Over the Rainbow." Yes, the movie is what matters. But the fact that you can play film historian for days on end while seeing the movie the way it was meant to be seen is weirdly subversive. Let the joyous news at last be spread: Ding-dong, VHS is dead.

2 A BUG'S LIFE COLLECTOR'S EDITION DVD *(Walt Disney/Pixar, G)* Or, as codirector Andrew Stanton calls this two-platter set, the "*soo-pah genius* version." And, by God, the man's not wrong. On one disc, you get the movie both in wide-screen and digitally altered to fill your TV. On the other disc, you get a bustling anthill of behind-the-scenes material that is—surprise!—as entertaining as the film. From the intentionally cheesy in-house presentation short *Fleabie* to testing sequences in which the characters' personalities evolve to revealed secrets of sound design, it's all here—linked by hilariously deadpan intros from Stanton, director John Lasseter, and others. For proof that making Pixar movies is as fun as watching them, skip to editor Lee Unkrich's discussion of the "progression demonstration"—while Lasseter and Stanton mime death-by-boredom behind him.

3 THE CELEBRATION *(PolyGram, R)* Even the directors who have signed on to Dogma 95 know that this Danish-bred statement of filmmaking principles is kind of a gimmick. It's all the more startling, then, that Thomas Vinterberg's blistering take on a family reunion soars beyond gimmickry, starting with the scene in which a son (Ulrich Thomsen) calmly toasts his father's birthday by telling the assembled guests of his childhood abuse at the hands of the old man. At first, no one is willing to believe him, but as familial complacency and complicity get peeled back, *Celebration* grows in power. And, no, it wouldn't have been half as good if shot un-Dogmatically.

4 BUFFALO '66 *(Universal, R)* The indie success story of 1998 (not released on tape until this year), it's still a too-little-seen gem. What sets Vincent Gallo apart from such bad-boy provocateurs as, say, Quentin Tarantino? If you can get beyond the look-at-me-Ma camera moves and the grimly hip scenario of a jailbird returning to his monstrous parents (Anjelica Huston and Ben Gazzara), you'll find a hero whose relationship with his kidnapped dream girl (Christina Ricci) becomes shockingly…tender. And how can you hate a guy who loves early Yes so much?

THE WIZARD OF OZ

this year's *Bringing Out the Dead*, in which director Martin Scorsese and writer Paul Schrader revisit the old nabe to diminishing returns). The DVD offers a splendidly deep, 70-minute behind-the-scenes documentary with contributions from parties expected (Scorsese, Schrader, Robert De Niro) and unexpected (Cybill Shepherd), yet the disc version is most compelling for the way it visually scrubs the old-movie patina off the murderous despair of Travis Bickle (De Niro), making it far easier to connect the dots to, say, schoolyard psychos of our here and now.

9 HENRY FOOL (*Columbia TriStar, R*) The classic that writer-director Hal Hartley was put on earth for, or merely the movie that makes his bohemians-in-suburbia posturing finally bearable? Depends on who you ask—but, since you're asking a guy who's been a follower since 1990's *The Unbelievable Truth* (and who has held on through the dark mid-'90s days of *Simple Men* and *Amateur*), *of course* it demands renting. You even get two stories for the price of one: the saga of a downtrodden garbageman (James Urbaniak) who finds sudden notoriety as a poet, and the complementary comedy of his blowhard artistic muse (Thomas Jay Ryan) who is revealed to be bereft of talent and must learn to live among mortals. Most films celebrate creativity—this one, remarkably, investigates what grows in its absence.

10 YELLOW SUBMARINE DVD (*MGM, G*) Since they spent all that money spiffing up the soundtrack and refurbishing the negative, doesn't revisiting Pepperland via VHS seem the height of perversity? DVD is the way you want to experience this flashback: The visuals are crystalline, the sound is a revelation, and extras include interviews with key personnel, storyboards for two never-filmed sequences, and alternate-track commentary by line producer John Coates. About the only voices missing from this project are those of Paul, George, and Ringo—but *Submarine* was always more about Beatles myth than reality.

5 THE DREAMLIFE OF ANGELS (*Columbia TriStar, R*) Most filmgoers weren't able to get to the few art houses playing this quietly devastating French movie; video, as usual, rides to the rescue by bringing the art house to them. At first, Erick Zonca's film seems a prosaic look at two young, working-class gal pals and their search for idle thrills. Slowly, though, the openhearted Isabelle (Élodie Bouchez) ascends toward grace as surely as cynical Marie (Natacha Regnier) tailspins into a ruinous relationship. Unexpectedly haunting, *Angels* is both a biography of a friendship and a map that charts the intersecting rise and fall of two casual seraphs.

6 THE MATRIX DVD (*Warner, R*) Welcome to the future. I'm not talking about the movie, which folds two decades of cyberpunk influences into a visually amazing whole that *still* doesn't transcend pulp. No, I'm talking about the *Matrix* DVD, which, when placed in the DVD-ROM drive of your computer, patches into the film's website for a freakily networked multimedia experience. This past Nov. 6, for instance, you could have watched the film on your PC while simultaneously partaking in a live chat with writer-directors Larry and Andy Wachowski. The implications are unnerving—imagine the movie-geek hive minds that could coalesce—and, in their own way, a hell of a lot more profound than anything Keanu Reeves is up to on screen.

7 KURT & COURTNEY (*BMG, R*) Nick Broomfield's documentary is about the John and Yoko of alterna rock. Actually, it's about the difficulty of making that documentary when Courtney Love is allegedly scaring off your financial backers. No, really, it's about the novel theory that Courtney had Kurt Cobain murdered. Then again, maybe it's just sour-grapes interviews with the losers scattered in Love's wake. Honestly, it's about Broomfield's search for the truth—*any* truth. Finally, it's about the impossibility of knowing.

8 TAXI DRIVER COLLECTOR'S EDITION DVD (*Columbia TriStar, R*) Twenty-three years on, *Taxi Driver* is a diorama of a brutal, bygone New York City—yet few museum pieces bite or bleed this ferociously (for proof, proceed to

A BUG'S LIFE

1

DIGITAL MUSIC

The threat was easy for the recording industry to dismiss when it was just kids pirating MP3 files. But then came the second wave: A horde of computer nerds stormed the green room and somehow convinced headliner acts like Alanis Morissette, David Bowie, and Metallica that traditional music distribution was as worn as a used eight-track tape. Legitimate digital-music distributors like Liquid Audio, EMusic.com, and Mjuice.com signed them up, followed by online record labels like Atomic Pop. The Diamond Rio portable MP3 player, fresh from winning a courtroom battle against the Recording Industry Association of America, was soon being imitated by such consumer-electronics powerhouses as Sony. And Internet music sales even earned their own *Billboard* music chart. On the downside, the music industry's attempt to have a secure digital-music format in place for Christmas failed, and the music-buying masses are getting fed up with a kajillion competing software players, formats, and prices. "I don't think this is going to break until the car-stereo revolution happens," says Ice-T, whose own label, Coroner Records, is now completely Internet based. But he still likens digital music to "a spaceship that's about to take off." And record labels that aren't on board will definitely be left behind.

2   **WWW.BLAIRWITCH.COM** The first time movie buff Jeff Johnson saw the *Blair Witch Project* website, he thought the story was real, just like everyone else. He paged through Maryland newspapers online, and even dispatched a query to the FBI's website. But after discovering he'd been duped, Johnson was less angered than impressed. "For me it wasn't about whether or not the movie was going to suck," says Johnson, 34. "It was about the whole spectacle that led up to it." The success of blairwitch.com immediately inspired imitators: Movies from *Fight Club* to *Scream 3* scrapped the traditional PR formula in favor of a stand-alone website. But translating *Witch*'s potent Web brew into box office dollars has proved a difficult trail to follow thus far.

3   **SHORT FILMS ON THE NET** "This is like the great billiard hall of bulls----ers," says former NBC prez Warren Littlefield. "The number of losers in all forms of entertainment are reborn with the Internet." True, but Littlefield—an adviser to the short-entertainment site AtomFilms *(www.atomfilms.com)*—also knows that with instant worldwide distribution and easy access to new talent, the number of winners on the Internet has increased as well. Among the people hoping to cash in are the founders of Pop.com, a website offering the short works of bigwigs like Steven Spielberg, Ron Howard, and Jeffrey Katzenberg. The upcoming year is looking like a long day at the movies for lunch-hour cinema lovers.

4   **PERSONAL VIDEO RECORDERS** If you had never commandeered a remote control, it would be hard to imagine that such a device could change your living-room habits. The same can be said of Personal Video Recorders, the new line of set-top boxes that let you pause *Who Wants to Be a Millionaire* in mid-Regis, or custom-create a channel full of *X-Files* episodes. With the help of ReplayTV, TiVo, or an EchoStar/WebTV combo, your prime time can be at 3 a.m. and filled with exactly the programs you want to watch. How will the networks cope with the time shift created by these newfangled VCRs? "One could argue that you actually increase the amount of viewing," says ReplayTV CEO Kim LeMasters, a former head of CBS Entertainment. Yeah, because you can finally fast-forward through the commercials.

AIBO

8 **SEGA DREAMCAST** If you think the Sega Dreamcast is just a temporary fix until the PlayStation 2 or the new Nintendo—code-named Dolphin—comes out next year, you haven't experienced the mind-numbing speed of *Sonic Adventure*, or the bone-crushing realism of *NFL 2K*. Dreamcast's built-in modem is also impressive—even if it only lets you post scores online—because it means you're getting the power of a desktop PC in a gaming machine that costs just $199. Sega, the videogame industry's perennial third-placer, mounted an impressive comeback in 1999, selling 514,000 consoles in two weeks alone. If new Dreamcast games keep pace, Sega might finally see its dreams come true.

9 **GOBLER TOYS** (*WWW.GOBLERTOYS.COM*) After reading the ad for Rodeo Rover ("Turns ordinary dogs into buckin' broncos!"), I revisited this website for "the greatest toys that never existed" countless times, hoping to find an online store that really did exist. But all I found in this virtual fun house were newer, more dangerous playthings from the devious minds of toy inventor Steve Casino and toy-industry product manager Steve Fink. Inspired by fictional 1940s-era toy magnate Ira Gobler, the site paints a Comedy Central-worthy corporate history that even includes theme music. In a year of great Web spoofs, this is the one that transported me to another, less sane reality.

10 **TIMOTHY MCSWEENEY'S INTERNET TENDENCY** (*WWW.MCSWEENEYS.NET*) Even though this Web magazine has been praised as *The New Yorker* of the Net, the literate and witty writers at *McSweeney's* would still like you to think they're obscure nobodies. Which explains the no-frills design, lackadaisical publishing schedule, and proofreading by "an unqualified person." What it doesn't explain is how 29-year-old founder Dave Eggers finds brilliant stories like Todd Pruzan's hot-tub limo adventure through Vegas; or Christina Nunez's highly literate reviews of random anecdotes she's heard recently; or Michael Genrich's deadpan comparison of lyrics by R&B artist Maxwell with the equations of Scottish scientist James Clerk Maxwell. This print quarterly with a website offshoot probably won't ever be flush with cash, but it's the salon du jour for tomorrow's literary stars—and something for readers to treasure while slurping the soup of the day.

5 **ENTERTAINMENT ROBOTS** When Terminators rule the world, what's left of the human race will recount stories of the day when an android was just a cute toy named Furby. They'll say that when Lego released the best-selling line of do-it-yourself MindStorms robot kits, it seemed like humans were still in control. But then Cye-sr, an $845 vacuum cleaner and delivery bot, started rolling around, and gadget-happy consumers lined up to pay $2,500 for a dog from Sony named AIBO. Even if the robot fad slackens, one thing has become clear: They'll be back.

6 **CELEBRITY AUCTIONS** Ally McBeal's pajamas—sold! *Titanic* life vest—sold! Autographed *Moesha* script—um, still available! Now studios have taken the next step on the e-commerce tie-in ladder and begun selling the name brands, like the Black Flys sunglasses used in *Blade*. With every vaguely entertainment-related item being peddled, however, the whole business is looking tarnished: One entrepreneur claimed to be selling the eggs of fashion models. There are some things money shouldn't buy.

7 **TOTALLY MAD** Before *Spy*, the *National Lampoon*, or *The Onion*, *MAD* magazine poked fun at everything this country held sacred. The result is nearly 50 years of smart-alecky humor—and now 564 back issues have been gloriously preserved by Brøderbund Software on seven CD-ROMs. From early TV parodies like "Dragged Net!" to such trademark features as "Spy vs. Spy," *MAD* has been a bad influence on generations of kids. *Totally MAD* is a perfect way to spread the "What, Me Worry?" virus to the next generation.

SEGA NFL 2K

BOWING OUT

STANLEY
KUBRICK

When Stanley Kubrick died of a heart attack in his sleep on March 7 at the age of 70—mere days after turning a print of his last film, *Eyes Wide Shut*, over to executives at Warner Bros.— there was the initial sense that his passing might be the final dark joke of a world-class pessimist. His reputation as a control freak was legendary: Tales abound of Kubrick putting actors through 100 takes of one shot, showing up at movie theaters in London's West End to make certain his films got the right sound and projection balance, orchestrating every last adverb of promotional copy. What better way to ensure massive interest in your first film in 12 years than to die? More rationally (but still tellingly), his death was the kind of psychic curveball that Kubrick specialized in throwing throughout his life. Where other directors hewed to specific genres, he roamed the cinematic landscape, covering satire (*Dr. Strangelove*), war (*Paths of Glory*, *Full Metal Jacket*), period drama (*Barry Lyndon*), epics (*Spartacus*), future shock (*A Clockwork Orange*), sci-fi profundity (*2001: A Space Odyssey*), and straight-up horror (*The Shining*). All that connected such shimmering dots was,

in the words of his biographer, Alexander Walker, the belief that men "are risen apes, not fallen angels." That cynicism was of a piece with Kubrick's times: He was America's most prominent contribution to the ranks of visionary postwar directors, on equal footing with Bergman and Kurosawa, Godard and Fellini. Of all their work, Kubrick's films stand out most like warning shots across the bow of human complacency, seeing civilization as a brittle veneer that constantly fails to keep savagery at bay.

Yes, *Eyes Wide Shut* turned out to be a disappointment—the work of a man too long closed off from the world (an expatriate, Kubrick had lived reclusively in and around London since the '60s). In a way, though, it was a homecoming. Born in the Bronx, having lifted himself through sheer ornery will out of a still-photography career and into filmmaking, Kubrick nevertheless made New York City the setting of his final film. It's a ghostly New York, though—created on British sets, eerily underpopulated, seen through the prisms of memory and dream. It is the ultimate work of a man who deeply distrusted humanity—yet who saw the ability to imagine as our lone saving grace. —*Ty Burr*

ALLEN FUNT

He was such an inveterate prankster even his death took a moment to sink in. When *Candid Camera* host Allen Funt, 84, passed away on Sept. 5 at his home in Pebble Beach, Calif., he took with him a legacy of elaborately choreographed practical jokes, devoted, as he once said, to catching people "in the act of being themselves." He will be remembered for one familiar phrase—"Smile! You're on *Candid Camera*!"—that may outlive us all. Funt was born in Brooklyn in 1914, the son of a Russian-born diamond importer. After attending Cornell, he worked in radio advertising, where he cultivated a special gift for gimmickry. In 1947, after a stint in Armed Forces Radio during World War II, Funt took a radio program he'd created called *Candid Microphone* to ABC, where it ran for less than a year before moving to NBC and changing its name to *Candid Camera*; he then took it to CBS in 1949. The show became one of the most popular on TV: It would air in various incarnations for more than 40 years with a range of cohosts, including Phyllis George and Loni Anderson. Today, Funt's influence can be seen in such derivative programs as *America's Funniest Home Videos*. Beyond *Candid Camera* (he last appeared on the show in 1990; his son, Peter, is now the cohost), Funt made seven comedy albums and wrote three books in a similar vein as his famous creation. And well before his own death, he created a charity called the Laughter Therapy Foundation, which distributes *Candid Camera* tapes to critically ill patients. Obviously, he was a man who truly believed laughter is the best medicine. —*Andrew Essex*

GEORGE C. SCOTT

His heart was in stage work—George C. Scott felt that his peak came as Shylock in 1962's *The Merchant of Venice*—but his monumental head seemed built for the screen. At any rate, the mind inside of it was inclined toward volatility and risk. He was a Hollywood heretic (calling the Oscars a "beauty contest in a slaughterhouse," refusing his Best Actor award for 1970's *Patton*) and a self-confessed madman (he said his life's work had psychologically scarred him). For Scott, who died of a ruptured aneurysm Sept. 22 at 71, acting was not merely a craft or a career, but an existential ordeal. As he once put it, "Acting was, in every sense, my means of survival." The grandest of his creations is Gen. George S. Patton—the actor doesn't portray the World War II commander so much as he plays host to storms of megalomania and melancholy. His other famous soldier is a player in World War III, Gen. "Buck" Turgidson of *Dr. Strangelove* (1964). Gung ho, cuckoo, apocalyptically slaphappy, his Turgidson is a triumph of mordant slapstick. Even in that comic role, Scott exudes a singular sense of danger, reminding us that he had the stuff to top the magnetism of movie gods: As a sharklike prosecutor in *Anatomy of a Murder* (1959), he steals scenes from Jimmy Stewart, and as a reptilian gambler in *The Hustler* (1961), he overpowers Paul Newman. The weapon of Scott's survival was a pure and animal ferocity. —*Troy Patterson*

DUSTY
SPRINGFIELD

Dusty Springfield, who succumbed to breast cancer March 2 at age 59 in her home in England's Henley-on-Thames, once said that she thought she was going to grow up to be a librarian. Though her name can be found in many books—often accompanied by phrases like "queen of white soul," as producer Jerry Wexler called her—fate had other plans for the smoky-voiced chanteuse. Born Mary Isobel Catherine Bernadette O'Brien, she adopted the Springfield moniker in the early '60s after leaving the folk trio the Springfields for a solo pop career. The giddy "I Only Want to Be With You," from 1964, was the first of a string of hits that also included "Wishin' and Hopin'" and "Stay Awhile." Her magnum opus, the 1969 album *Dusty in Memphis*,

still stands as a landmark, a critically acclaimed touchstone that continues to inspire singers. Springfield, who battled depression and substance abuse, had been in semiretirement since the early '70s, but she always had high-profile supporters. In 1987, she collaborated with the Pet Shop Boys on "What Have I Done to Deserve This?" and director Quentin Tarantino used her "Son of a Preacher Man" in a pivotal scene from *Pulp Fiction*. Though she kept her lesbianism a secret, she was, appropriately, inducted into the Rock and Roll Hall of Fame this year by outspoken homosexual Elton John. "Hers was the first fan club I belonged to," John has said. "I had pictures of Dusty all over my walls." All in all, hardly a dusty legacy. —*Tom Sinclair*

GENE
SISKEL

Gene Siskel's favorite movie was *Saturday Night Fever*. He saw it 17 times when it first opened, bought John Travolta's trademark white suit at auction, and referred to his taste for the film as a "visceral attachment." His sparring partner, Roger Ebert, once connected that visceral attachment to the dancing passion of Travolta's Tony Manero by way of one of Siskel's personal mottos: "Devote your life to something you love—not like, but *love*." Of course, the love of Siskel's life—which ended Feb. 20 at age 53, nine months after brain surgery—was the movies. In 1975, six years after becoming the film critic for the *Chicago Tribune*, he teamed up with Ebert, his rival at the *Chicago Sun-Times*, to create *Opening Soon at a Theater Near You*. Over the years, as that local PBS show grew into a nationally syndicated sensation titled *Siskel & Ebert*, the hosts single-handedly—or, rather, double-thumbedly—came to shape popular film criticism. Zesty, direct, colorfully concise, the "Sisbert" style is the rhetorical equivalent of *Fever*'s serio-disco coming-of-age tale. The show is both pop and populist—appreciative of sharp fun, sensitive to vernacular style, and gracious in using its influence to make art-house hits of films like *My Dinner With André* and *Hoop Dreams*. With Siskel gone, the program (retitled *Roger Ebert & the Movies*) now costars a rotating array of guest reviewers, many of whom "the skinny guy" could claim as heirs. His show goes on. —*TP*

MARIO PUZO

Without him, there would have been no Sonny, no Michael, no Fredo, not a lone Corleone, and certainly no jowly Marlon Brando. Mario Puzo, who died on July 2 at age 78 of heart failure in his Long Island, N.Y., home, was our preeminent chronicler of the Cosa Nostra. Puzo's vivid imagination gave birth to the Mafia epic known as *The Godfather*, a literary phenomenon that would spend 67 weeks on the *New York Times* bestseller list, sell 21 million copies worldwide, and sire not one but two Oscar-winning films—for which Puzo coauthored screenplays with director Francis Ford Coppola. Puzo's life began in suitable cinematic fashion on the mean streets of New York City's Hell's Kitchen, where he was one of seven children born to Italian immigrants from Naples (not Sicily). His first two novels were commercial flops. *The Godfather* was turned down by several publishers, then Putnam accepted it for a $5,000 advance. Though Puzo's work almost single-handedly elevated the dark side of the Italian-American experience into American myth ("an offer he can't refuse" is now included in *Bartlett's Familiar Quotations*), some saw larger themes in his work. Writer Gay Talese said *The Godfather* "emphasized the importance of family, the ideal of fidelity of family, and vengeful reaction to those who are disloyal." Admirers believed that Puzo's ability to write so convincingly about the Mob came from actual experience, but the author insisted he learned everything from research, declaring in a 1997 interview, "I hate violence." —*AE*

JOE DiMAGGIO

When all is said and done, what did he really *do*? Well, he played brilliant, subtle, thoroughbred baseball from 1936 until 1951. He married Marilyn Monroe in 1954; they divorced after nine fractious months. And he was reinvented as a product pitchman (most notably in spots for Mr. Coffee) in the 1960s. But what did Joe DiMaggio, who died March 8 of cancer at the age of 84, do for us recently? Why, 45 years after his last major pop-culture moment, did grown men weep at the news of his death?

Because of what he didn't do. Talk.

How incomprehensibly rare is that in this age of 500-channel, 24-7, dorm-cam ego-ubiquity? Enough so that crowds parted, in theory and in fact, before the Yankee Clipper's graceful reticence. On the field or in the headlines, he conveyed the idea that what mattered was only what you did. How you felt about it was nobody's business but your own. The son of an immigrant fisherman from Sicily, DiMaggio played center field for the New York Yankees like a casual god. His 56-game hitting streak in 1941 remains an untouchable record; less noted are his jaw-droppingly low 369 lifetime strikeouts. Baseball is rarely an arena of class, Hollywood even less so; his attempt to ground Monroe's needy exuberance might have been a fool's errand, but its failure only gave his reserve a wounded, noble air. By 1967, in the lyrics to "Mrs. Robinson," Paul Simon would be wondering where he had gone, plaintively holding up "Joltin' Joe" as the last American hero. By the time of his death, DiMaggio would be something far more unusual: the last private man. —*TB*

MEL
TORME

Mel Tormé found his calling early. The crooner known as the Velvet Fog, who died June 5 at age 73 in L.A of complications from a past stroke, began singing professionally at age 4, after being invited to sit in with the band at a Chicago restaurant/nightclub. Young Mel's vocal prowess so impressed the management, they hired him to sing for $15 a week, and he never looked back. In the ensuing years, Tormé would make his musical mark on a number of fronts. He was one of the premier pop crooners and jazz vocalists of the '40s and '50s, and an acknowledged master of the free-form singing style known as scatting. He was also a talented songwriter who coauthored the oft-recorded holiday standard "The Christmas Song (Chestnuts Roasting on an Open Fire)". As singer Ethel Waters once said, "Mel Tormé is the only white man who sings with the soul of a black man." Though rock & roll slowed his career in the '60s, he had an upswing in the '70s, and the '90s lounge-music revival recast Tormé as a hip elder statesman; he appeared on MTV, in *The Naked Gun 2 1/2: The Smell of Fear*, and guested on *Seinfeld*. In February, Tormé received a Lifetime Achievement Award at the 1999 Grammy Awards. Whether his smooth singing style was in or out of fashion, his huskily emotive baritone always remained an exquisite instrument. In the end, precious few vocalists of any generation could cut the Velvet Fog. —*TS*

DAVID
STRICKLAND

In his career, David Strickland may have been relegated to supporting status—he was an endearingly boyish music scribe on NBC's Brooke Shields vehicle *Suddenly Susan* and a lovelorn loser in the Ben Affleck–Sandra Bullock romance *Forces of Nature*—but he had a starring role in a tormented real-life drama that abruptly ended March 22 when he hanged himself with a bedsheet in a seedy Las Vegas hotel. Diagnosed as manic depressive the year before, the 29-year-old actor had long battled alcoholism and drug abuse (the day he died, Strickland was due to appear in an L.A. court to demonstrate that he had remained drug-free after an arrest on cocaine possession charges the previous October), and had even made an earlier suicide attempt in 1998. Still, things seemed to be looking up in the days before Strickland's fateful trip to Vegas. Despite mediocre ratings, *Susan* had been renewed for a fourth season, and *Forces*, his first major studio movie, had just topped the box office. What's more, he had a steady girlfriend in *Beverly Hills, 90210* grad Tiffani-Amber Thiessen. "I was really comforted by the fact that everything was going so well," *Susan* costar Nestor Carbonell recently told *20/20*. "Unfortunately, it proved to be the calm before the storm." Indeed it was. Earlier in the year, Strickland had stopped taking the lithium prescribed for his manic depression. The weekend of his death, he met up in L.A. with *NewsRadio* star—and fellow party boy—Andy Dick, going with him to a Vegas club, Girls of Glitter Gulch, on Sunday. Later that night, according to police, Strickland was solo when he checked into Vegas' Oasis motel, polished off a six-pack of beer, and took his life. "He wanted so badly to be able to handle his success," Carbonell has said. Sadly, it was not to be. —*Shawna Malcom*

HUNTZ HALL

In a more innocent time, he was juvenile delinquency's dopey sidekick—rubber-faced and gawky, the brim of his cap turned upward in defiance (or maybe in silliness). Henry "Huntz" Hall was a member of the boys' clubs that made up "youth films" of the 1930s, '40s, and '50s—the Dead End Kids, the East Side Kids, the Bowery Boys—yet there was nothing delinquent about his pro-fessionalism. That's because Hall, one of 14 children born to an immigrant Irish engineer, spent his boyhood performing in vaudeville and radio serials. In 1935 he played "Dippy" to Leo Gorcey's "Spit" in Broadway's *Dead End*; two years later, Hall, a 16-year-old New York City boy through and through, moved to Hollywood to make the film version, which costarred Humphrey Bogart. *Angels With Dirty Faces*, *Crime School*, and *Spooks Run Wild* followed. After the gangs' run of over 85 films (the final one was released in 1958), he acted sporadically, but even when he died in L.A. on Jan. 30, at age 78, Hall was branded by his youthful image. He was still an angel with a dirty face. —*Joe Neumaier*

VICTOR MATURE

He was associated with phrases like *broad-shouldered*, *beefcake*, *brawny*, and *hunk*. Yet by any description, Victor Mature, who died of cancer on Aug. 4, at 86, was a presence in Hollywood. He made films in many genres during the '40s and '50s—like the gangster noir *Kiss of Death* and John Ford's classic Western *My Darling Clementine*, in which he played the brooding Doc Holliday to Henry Fonda's squeaky-clean Wyatt Earp—but Mature was best known for sword-and-sandal epics like *The Robe*, *Androcles and the Lion*, *Demetrius and the Gladiators*, and, of course, *Samson and Delilah*; the biblical strongman became his signature role. Mature combined Tyrone Power's brooding with Tarzan's physique, and it paid off. The actor was regarded as something like the thinking man's he-man—an image he good-naturedly aped in '60s farces like *After the Fox* and the Monkees' druggy film lark, *Head*. But Mature was no fool: After several years away from the screen, he returned to play Samson's father in the 1984 TV movie *Samson and Delilah*. He'd be damned if someone filmed that particular biblical tale without him. —*JN*

SYLVIA
SIDNEY

Sylvia Sidney's first film role was as herself, in 1927's *Broadway Nights*. More than 70 years later, in some of her final parts, she could have been billed the same way. By the time Sidney, who died July 1 at 88 of complications from throat cancer, appeared in two Tim Burton films—*Beetlejuice* (1988) and *Mars Attacks!* (1996)—her raspy voice and extra-tart delivery were instantly recognizable. In the '30s, Sidney was one of Paramount's top starlets; later, she starred in Alfred Hitchcock's *Sabotage* (1936), as well as Fritz Lang's *Fury* (1936) and *You Only Live Once* (1937). But her famous offscreen temper and love of the stage soon led her back to the theater in the 1940s. In Hollywood, Sidney noted, "I didn't know who I was, as an actress or a person." But Broadway knew who she was: a star, especially in 1941's thriller *Angel Street* and Irwin Shaw's *The Gentle People*. Nonetheless, she continued in TV and in films through her golden years, winning a Golden Globe for the 1985 AIDS drama *An Early Frost*. In her final months, she appeared as an otherworldly travel agent on ABC's revamped *Fantasy Island*. She also wrote books on her non-acting passion: needlepoint, which was appropriate. After all, few in Hollywood were so dependably sharp. —*JN*

OLIVER
REED

The gruff-and-tumble characters Oliver Reed brought to oversize life on screen could be brutish burglars (1968's *Oliver!*, directed by his uncle, Carol Reed), caddish husbands (1969's *Women in Love*), cruel father figures (1975's *Tommy*), or even literal monsters (1961's Hammer horror flick *Curse of the Werewolf*, his starring debut). But even among this rogues' gallery, the Wimbledon-born actor's devilish smile and engaging presence could make an audience warm to him. However, in real life, Reed, who died at age 61 on May 2 of a heart attack while making a movie on the island of Malta, had quite the reputation for brawling and a volcanic temper. ("I'm not a villain," he once remarked. "I'm just a tawdry character who explodes now and again.") And his British bar manners could sometimes resemble those of his Athos from 1973's *The Three Musketeers* and 1975's *The Four Musketeers*; indeed, Reed once bragged of drinking over a hundred pints of beer in 24 hours. But this onetime bouncer and boxer used his bearish quality to such impressive effect, it was often hard to tell where the real Reed ended and his screen persona began. Most likely, that was all part of his wicked plan. —*JN*

DANA PLATO

It's been called the *Diff'rent Strokes* curse, and no one suffered it quite so badly as actress Dana Plato. On May 8—some 15 years after her *Strokes* character, Kimberly Drummond, was written out of the popular NBC sitcom because the actress had become pregnant—Plato was found dead in her Winnebago, which was parked outside the Moore, Okla., home of her fiancé's parents. Local police attributed her death to an accidental overdose of Valium and the painkiller Loritab (Plato had recently appeared on Howard Stern's radio program to refute claims that she was using drugs). She was 34 years old, and is survived by a son, Tyler Lambert, 15.

It was a sad end to her promising showbiz career, which began when she was 6 with a series of films and television commercials, continued on *Strokes*—and ended with straight-to-video schlock, a 1989 nude *Playboy* layout, and two five-year probation sentences after her notorious 1991 robbery of a Las Vegas video store and a 1992 prescription forgery for Valium. Perhaps it's best to remember Plato as the earnest stepsister to adopted brothers Arnold (Gary Coleman) and Willis (Todd Bridges). During the brief time she was a part of it, from 1978 to '84, *Strokes'* interracial family represented our amazing ability to withstand adversity. Too bad it was merely a TV fantasy. —*AE*

DEFOREST KELLEY

Growing up in Atlanta in the 1920s, DeForest Kelley, who died after a long illness on June 11, in Woodland Hills, Calif., at age 79, wanted to be a doctor. His family couldn't afford the schooling, but he would, eventually, get a medical degree—in the 23rd century, as the U.S.S. *Enterprise*'s chief medical officer, Leonard "Bones" McCoy, on *Star Trek*. The show's creator, Gene Roddenberry, famously described *Trek* as "*Wagon Train* to the stars." Fitting, then, that he should cast Kelley, whose laconic drawl served him well on TV Westerns including *Gunsmoke* and *Bonanza*, and opposite Burt Lancaster and Kirk Douglas in 1957's *Gunfight at the O.K. Corral*. Over three TV seasons (1966–69) and in six feature films (1979–91), Kelley proved to be the stabilizing element of the original *Trek*'s central trio: The down-home crustiness of his country doctor was the ideal foil for both the earnest courage of William Shatner's Captain Kirk and the glacial intellect of Leonard Nimoy's Mr. Spock. It's telling of Kelley's peculiar gravity that at news of his death, *Trek* aficionados could not resist the gallows humor of quoting his most famous phrase: "He's dead, Jim." For 33 years, Kelley lived in the shadow of McCoy, but it didn't bother him a whit. "*Star Trek* has been cream in the coffee to me," he once said. In paying tribute to Kelley, Nimoy noted that his friend "represented humanity, and it fitted him well. He was a decent, loving, caring partner." In other words, he lived long and he prospered. —*TP*

DIRK
BOGARDE

He embodied European decadence in films like 1971's *Death in Venice*, but earlier in his career, Dirk Bogarde's charm earned him the nickname "the British Rock Hudson." London-born Derek Jules Gaspard Ulric Niven van den Bogaerde played in thrillers and dramas as well as in farcical comedies (like 1954's *Doctor in the House*), becoming the U.K.'s top box office star in the late '50s. Bogarde, who died May 8 at age 78 of a heart attack, even helped launch Brigitte Bardot by choosing her for *Doctor at Sea* (1955). After trying Hollywood melodramas, the actor, discreetly gay in real life, became one of the first stars to play a homosexual character, a blackmailed lawyer, in the controversial British film *Victim* (1961). He later costarred with Julie Christie in 1965's swingin'-London drama *Darling*. But it was his role as a dying composer sadly obsessed with a young boy in *Death in Venice* that Bogarde considered his peak, his finely aged allure exemplifying faded aristocracy. As he acted less and turned to writing best-selling memoirs like *For the Time Being*, Bogarde became a symbol of a time when courtliness was the norm. —*JN*

MADELINE
KAHN

Not since Carole Lombard and Judy Holliday had anyone made sexy as funny as Madeline Kahn. Even her character names attest to it: exotic dancer Trixie Delight in *Paper Moon*, saloon singer Lili Von Shtüpp in *Blazing Saddles*, ditsy matron Gorgeous Teitelbaum in Broadway's *The Sisters Rosensweig*. And so do the cluster of classics (including *Young Frankenstein* and *What's Up, Doc?*) in which she batted her eyes, tossed back her hair, and cracked us up. When she died Dec. 3 at 57 from ovarian cancer, Kahn was a kook emeritus, a trouper who, after an education in speech therapy and training as an opera singer, cut her teeth on Broadway, then hit the movies in 1972 with *Doc*. But that background may have come in handy: She often imbued her campy vamps with nasally squeals, girlish lisps, and tigress-like growls. She earned Best Supporting Actress nominations two years in a row, for *Moon* (1973) and *Saddles* (1974)—the latter highlighted by Kahn's hilariously silly Marlene Dietrich send-up "I'm Tired." A 1983 sitcom, *Oh Madeline*, failed, but in 1993 *Sisters Rosensweig* nabbed her a Tony for Best Actress. Of late, she had appeared on CBS' *Cosby*, and her final role was in the indie flick *Judy Berlin*. Kahn didn't speak about her illness until just before her death, hoping her voice would raise awareness of the disease. "Laughter is [strange]. I mean, what is it?" she once mused. "It's some sort of explosive reaction." And one that always seemed to follow her. —*JN*

SANDRA GOULD

ALICE ADAMS, 72, novelist (*Superior Women*). May 27

JOEY ADAMS, 88, borscht-belt jokester and syndicated columnist. Dec. 2

KIRK ALYN, 88, first actor to play Superman in two movie serials. March 14

HOYT AXTON, 61, singer, songwriter (Three Dog Night's "Joy to the World"), actor (*Gremlins*). Oct. 26

IAN BANNEN, 71, theater and film actor (*Waking Ned Devine*). Nov. 3

LIONEL BART, 68, composer, librettist, and lyricist of Broadway's *Oliver!* April 3

WILLIAM BENEDICT, 82, actor in the Bowery Boys films of the '40s and '50s. Nov. 25

MARY KAY BERGMAN, 38, actress and voice of several female characters on the cartoon series *South Park*. Nov. 11

PAUL BOWLES, 88, writer (*The Shelter-*

QUENTIN CRISP

ing Sky), composer. Nov. 18

BOXCAR WILLIE (A.K.A. LECIL TRAVIS MARTIN), 67, country star and *Hee Haw* regular. April 12

HILLARY BROOKE, 84, actress (*The Philadelphia Story*). May 25

RORY CALHOUN, 76, movie and TV Western star (CBS' *The Texan*). April 28

ALLAN CARR, 62, Tony award-winning Broadway (*La Cage aux Folles*) and film (*Grease*) producer. June 29

ANITA CARTER, 66, country singer and bass player who was a member of the famed Carter Family. July 29

PEGGY CASS, 74, Tony award-winning actress (*Auntie Mame*), and game- and talk-show regular (*To Tell the Truth, The Jack Paar Show*). March 8

WILT "THE STILT" CHAMBERLAIN, 63, basketball legend and author of the notorious autobiography *A View From Above: Sports, Sex, and Controversy*. Oct. 12

DEL CLOSE, 64, improv comedian, came up with the idea for *SCTV*. March 4

IRON EYES CODY, 94, veteran Native American actor best known for a public service ad in which he shed a tear over the sight of a polluted America. Jan. 4

ELLEN CORBY, 87, character actress best known for playing Grandma on TV's *The Waltons*. April 14

CHARLES CRICHTON, 89, comedy director (*The Lavender Hill Mob, A Fish Called Wanda*). Sept. 14

QUENTIN CRISP, 90, eccentric gay writer (*The Naked Civil Servant*) and actor (*Orlando*). Nov. 21

RICK DANKO, 56, bassist and singer with the seminal '60s group The Band. Dec. 10

JIMMY DAY, 65, famed pedal steel guitarist. Jan. 22

FRANK DEVOL, 88, composer. He penned the hummable themes to TV's *Brady Bunch* and *My Three Sons*. Oct. 27

EDWARD DMYTRYK, 90, director (*Murder, My Sweet; The Caine Mutiny*) and member of the blacklisted Hollywood Ten. July 1

HARRY "SWEETS" EDISON, 83, jazz trumpeter for the Count Basie band. July 27

BETTY LOU GERSON, 84, voiced Cruella De Vil in Disney's 1961 animated *101 Dalmatians*. Jan. 12

SANDRA GOULD, 73, character actress who played busybody Gladys Kravitz on TV's *Bewitched*. She also appeared on *I Love Lucy* and *My Three Sons*. July 20

RONNY GRAHAM, 79, comic actor-writer who collaborated with Mel Brooks on such films as *To Be or Not to Be* and *Spaceballs*. He also wrote for TV's *M*A*S*H*. July 4

JOSEPH HELLER, 76, author of the classic World War II novel *Catch-22*. Dec. 12

ANTHONY NEWLEY

SHIRLEY HEMPHILL, 52, actress, played a waitress on TV's *What's Happening!!*. Dec. 10

BOB HERBERT, 57, music manager and cocreator of the Spice Girls. Aug. 9

ED HERLIHY, 89, radio announcer, actor, voice of Kraft Foods for four decades. Jan. 30

GEORGE V. HIGGINS, 59, crime novelist (*The Friends of Eddie Coyle*). Nov. 6

AL HIRT, 76, pop-jazz trumpeter who received eight Grammy nominations, and won in 1963 for "Java." April 27

SEÑOR WENCES

HORST P. HORST, 93, photographer whose fashion portraits and ad work influenced celebrity pictures and pop images. Nov. 18

MILT JACKSON, 76, vibraphonist, founding member of the Modern Jazz Quartet. Oct. 9

BRION JAMES, 54, character actor (*Blade Runner*). Aug. 7

HENRY JONES, 86, character actor. Played the eerie handyman in the Broadway and Hollywood versions of *The Bad Seed*. May 17

GARSON KANIN, 86, writer-director of Broadway shows (*Born Yesterday*, *Funny Girl*) and films (*Adam's Rib*, *Pat and Mike*). March 13

RICHARD KILEY, 76, Tony award-winning actor who created the role of Don Quixote in Broadway's *Man of La Mancha*. March 5

MABEL KING, 66, actress, played the Witch Evillene in Broadway's *The Wiz*. Nov. 9

HERBERT KLINE, 89, Oscar-nominated documentary director of *Lights Out in Europe*. Feb. 5

LUCILLE LORTEL, 98, legendary Off Broadway arts patron who founded the Lucille Lortel Theatre in Manhattan. April 4

ROBERT "GORILLA MONSOON" MARELLA, 62, professional wrestler. Oct. 6

DONAL McCANN, 56, noted Irish dramatic actor (*Stealing Beauty*). July 17

LORD YEHUDI MENUHIN, 82, one of the century's great violin virtuosos. March 12

DONALD MILLS, 84, singer with the famed Mills Brothers. Nov. 13

AKIO MORITA, 78, cofounder and former chairman of the Sony Corp. Oct. 3

GARY MORTON, 74, comedian and TV producer, husband of Lucille Ball. March 30

DAME IRIS MURDOCH, 79, philosopher-novelist (*The Sea, the Sea*). Feb. 8

ANTHONY NEWLEY, 67, actor-singer-songwriter, costarred in 1967's *Doctor Dolittle*, cowrote the music for 1971's *Willy Wonka and the Chocolate Factory* (which spawned Sammy Davis Jr.'s hit "The Candy Man"), and cocreated and starred in Broadway's *Stop the World—I Want to Get Off*. April 14

RED NORVO, 91, jazz musician. April 6

JENNIFER PATERSON, 71, cohost of the Food Network's *Two Fat Ladies*. Aug. 10

SUSAN STRASBERG

NOAM PITLIK, 66, TV and film actor (*The Graduate*), Emmy award-winning TV director (*Barney Miller*, *Taxi*). Feb. 18

GENE RAYBURN, 81, TV and radio personality, host of *The Match Game*. Nov. 29

BERT REMSEN, 78, character actor (*Pork Chop Hill*, *Forces of Nature*). April 22

NANCY RICHARDS-AKERS, 45, romance novelist (*Wild Irish Skies*). June 5

CHARLES "BUDDY" ROGERS, 94, film actor (*Wings*, *My Best Girl*). April 21

OSCAR SCAGGS, 21, soundman and son of musician Boz Scaggs. Dec. 31

WALTER SCOTT, 84, former NBC chairman who, in 1965, made the decision to broadcast the entire NBC schedule in color. March 12

BOBBY SHEEHAN, 31, founding member of and bassist for Blues Traveler. Aug. 20

JEAN SHEPHERD, 78, radio host, author of *In God We Trust, All Others Pay Cash* (basis for the film *A Christmas Story*). Oct. 16

SHEL SILVERSTEIN, 68, author and illustrator of such children's favorites as *A Light in the Attic* and *Where the Sidewalk Ends*, and lyricist-composer, notably of Johnny Cash's 1969 hit "A Boy Named Sue." May 10

SKIP SPENCE, 52, founding member of the rock group Jefferson Airplane. April 16

SAUL STEINBERG, 84, cartoonist whose work was seen in *The New Yorker*. May 12

JESSE STONE, 97, composer, lyricist, and arranger ("Shake, Rattle and Roll"). April 1

SUSAN STRASBERG, 60, daughter of acting teacher Lee Strasberg and a Broadway star at 17 playing Anne Frank. She also appeared in *Picnic* and *Stage Struck*. Jan. 21

BOBBY TROUP, 80, songwriter and actor whose claim to fame was "(Get Your Kicks On) Route 66." Feb. 7

SEÑOR WENCES, 103, Spanish-born ventriloquist. Appeared on *The Ed Sullivan Show* with his characters Johnny the "hand" puppet and Pedro the head in a box, whose trademark "S'all right? S'all right" became a catchphrase. April 20

NORMAN WEXLER, 73, screenwriter of *Saturday Night Fever* and *Serpico*. Aug. 23

ERNIE WISE, 73, British comic. March 21

ELLEN CORBY

SOFT COVER Roberts: Photograph by Matthew Rolston; Martin: Jim Wright/Icon; *The Sopranos*: Photograph by Michael O'Neill; Myers: Photograph by Kate Garner. **HARDCOVER** *Sopranos*: Photograph by Michael O'Neill; Roberts, Locklear: Photographs by Matthew Rolston; *Austin Powers*: E. J. Camp; Gellar, Reeves: Photographs by Moshe Brakha; the Dixie Chicks: Photograph by Jeffrey Thurnher; Osment: Photograph by Mojgan B. Azimi; Messing and McCormack: Photograph by Robert Trachtenberg; Martin: Pablo Alfaro/Botaish Group. ENTERTAINERS OF THE YEAR Martin: Pablo Alfaro/Botaish Group; Spears: Jon Ragel/Corbis Outline; Roberts: Brigitte Lacombe; Santana: Jay Blakesberg; Washington: George Lange/Corbis Outline; Jonze: Silvia Otte. **BREAKOUT STARS** Bentley:'s styling: Alejandro Peraza/Celestine; grooming: Robert Steinken/Celestine; shirt: Emporio Armani. Meloni's styling: Silvia Ryder/Celestine; grooming: Colleen Campbell/Profile; shirt: Prada/Neiman Marcus. Stiles: Rafael Fuchs/Corbis Outline. Moss: Davis Factor/Corbis Outline. *American Pie* cast's styling: Danny Flynn/Cloutier; hair: Alex Dizon/Artists, Keiko/Celestine; makeup: Kimber/Artist Group Management, Lynn Taylor/Rex; grooming: Debra Furello/Artists, Charlotte/Artists; men's clothing: American Rag; women's dresses: Wasteland; jewelry: Tarina Tarantino. Bank: Ethan Hill. GREAT PERFORMANCES Cusack: Brigitte Lacombe. Stewart: Frank W. Ockenfels 3/Corbis Outline. Cher: Michael Lavine/Corbis Outline. Northam: Leslie Hassler/Corbis Outline. Russo: Mark Liddell/Icon. Wahlberg's styling: Deborah Waknin/Celestine; hair: Johnny Villanueva/Artists; makeup: Deborah J. Mowat; shirt: John Bartlett; pants: Agnes B. Eisenberg. Levy: Vivian Zink. *South Park: Bigger, Longer & Uncut*: Paramount. **YEAR IN REVIEW** Matenopoulos: Lawrence Schwartzwald/Liaison Agency; *The View*: Steve Fenn. Clooney: Michael O'Neill/Corbis Outline. Rodman: Suzette Bross/London Features. Anderson Lee: David Fisher/London Features. Benigni at Oscars: Michael Caulfield/AP/Wide World; Davis, Ford: Academy of Motion Picture Arts and Sciences; Spielberg: Reuters/Gary Hershorn/Archive Photos; Redgrave and Condon: Lucy Nicholson/AFP Photo/Corbis. Sawyer: Jonathan Exley. Teletubbies: Ragdoll Productions/AP/Wide World. Blaine: Andrea Renault/Globe Photos. Lewinsky on *20/20*: IPOL (4). Hill: Reed Saxon/AP/Wide World. *Death of a Salesman*: Eric Y. Exit/The Goodman Theatre; *Iceman Cometh*: Joan Marcus. Combs: Lynsey Addario/AP/Wide World. Pope: Ira Wyman/Corbis Sygma. Yoda in *Phantom Menace*: ©Lucasfilm Ltd. & TM. Fabio: Roger Karnbad/Celebrity Photo. *The Simpsons*: The Simpsons TM & ©1998 20th Century Fox Film Corp. Littleton crosses: Michael S. Green/AP/Wide World; mourners: Ron Chenoy/Sipa Press; kids: Hal Stoelzle/Rocky Mountain News/Corbis Sygma; Manson: Rune Hellestad/Corbis. *The Beach*: Peter Mountain. Camp: Jeff Slocomb/Corbis Outline. *Phantom Menace*: Keith Hamshere ©Lucasfilm Ltd. & TM; *Menace* ticket holder: Chris Pizzello/AP/Wide World; *Menace* fans: Mike Segar/Reuters/Archive Photos; *Menace* fans sleeping: Mary Ann Chastain/AP/Wide World; Lucci *Post* cover: Photograph by Anthony Verde. Fisher: David Duprey/AP/Wide World. Turlington: Steve Sands/Corbis Outline. *Seinfeld* Soup Nazi: Joey Del Valle. Depp: Axel Groussett/UGR/London Features. Speedman: James Sorenson; Foley: Andrew Eccles; Jackson: Uwe Lein/AP/Wide World. *Tarzan*: Edgar Rice Burroughs, Inc./Disney. Kennedy and Bessette (formal), Kennedy and Bessette (boat), Coast Guard: Kevin Wisniewski/REX USA; mourners: Allan Tannenbaum/Corbis Sygma; note: Les Stone/Corbis Sygma. Manheim: Mark Lennihan/AP/Wide World. Springsteen, fans: Kevin Mazur (2). Jagger and Hall: Hudson/Corbis Outline. Gumbel: Tony Esparza. Woodstock diver, rioting, Jewel, Kid Rock: Frank Micelotta/ImageDirect (4). Kiss: Barry Levine. *Austin Powers*:

Kimberly Wright. Ross: Adam Butler/AP/Wide World. (*SNL* party) Kattan, Lovitz, Hanks: Dave Allocca/DMI; Goodman and Crystal, Myers and Spade: DMI (2); Shannon and Barrymore: Andrea Renault/Globe Photos; *Once and Again*: Ron Tom. Moore: Marty Lederhandler/AP/Wide World. Jackson and Rowe: Ed/Ho Businesswire/Reuters. Sklar and Seinfeld: Lawrence Schwartzwald/Liaison Agency; *Toy Story 2*: ©Disney/Pixar; *Pokémon*: Nintendo (9). *Green Mile*: Ralph Nelson. *American Beauty*: Lorey Sebastian. *Angela's Ashes*: David Appleby. Pitt and Aniston: Keith Butler/Online USA. *X-Files*: Michael Lavine. Lopez: Frank Micelotta/ImageDirect; Snoopy: United Features Syndicate. **YEAR IN PICTURES** *Man on the Moon*: Francois Duhamel; *Anna and the King, Talented Mr. Ripley*: Brigitte Lacombe; *Buffy*: Richard Cartwright. **STYLE Gellar:** Kathy Hutchins/Hutchins Photo (large photo); John Spellman/Retna (*Divas* concert); Jim Smeal/Galella, Ltd. (WB press tour); Jen Lombardo/Mazur (*SNL* party). **Zeta-Jones:** Jean-Pierre Amet/Corbis Sygma (large photo); Scott Downie/Celebrity Photo (Oscars); Daniel Dyson/Camera Press/Retna (airport). **Theron:** Gilbert Flores/Celebrity Photo (large photo); Jim Smeal/Galella, Ltd. (Fire & Ice ball); Andrea Renault/Globe Photos (Oscar party). **Hurley:** Brendan Beirne/Corbis Sygma (large photo); Jim Smeal/Galella, Ltd. (*Mickey* premiere); John Spellman/Retna (NYC premiere); Kevin Mazur (fashion gala). **Roberts:** Kevin Mazur (large photo); Gregory Pace/Corbis Sygma (*Notting* premiere); Frank Trapper/Corbis Sygma (*Bride* premiere). **Russo:** Jeff Kravitz/Film Magic (large photo); Ronald Siemoneit/Corbis Sygma (Berlin premiere); Dennis Van Tine/London Features (*Crown* premiere); Kevin Mazur (fashion awards). **Lopez:** Gilbert Flores/Celebrity Photo (large photo); Gregory Pace/Corbis Sygma (in Gucci); Jen Lombardo/Mazur (MTV awards). **Paltrow:** Nina Prommer/Globe Photos (large picture); Fitzroy Barrett/Globe Photos (Golden Globes); Bill Davila/Retna (*Shakespeare* premiere). **Russell:** Ron Davis/Shooting Star (large picture); Kevin Winter/Celebrity Photo (MTV awards); Fitzroy Barrett/Globe Photos (Golden Globes). **TLC:** Bob Beccaris/Mazur (large picture); Steve Granitz/Retna (Lopes alone); Kevin Mazur (MTV awards). BEST & WORST (**Movies**) *Man on the Moon*: Francois Duhamel; *Election*: Photofest; *Being John Malkovich*: Melissa Moseley; *Boys Don't Cry*: Bill Matlock; *Run Lola Run*: Bernd Spauke; *Dogma*: Darren Michaels; *Double Jeopardy*: Ron McEwan. (**Video**) *Wizard of Oz*: MGM/MPTV; *Wizard of Oz* (shoes): Photofest; *A Bug's Life*: Photofest. (**TV**) *Now and Again*: Dennis Haysbert; *The X-Files*: Nicola Goode; *The Sopranos*: Anthony Neste; *The Simpsons*: The Simpsons TM & ©1999 20th Century Fox Film Corp.; *Buffy*: Richard Cartwright; *Freaks and Geeks*: Chris Haston. (**Books**) Englander: Photograph by Ethan Hill; *Close Range* cover: Photograph by Anthony Verde. (**Music**) Williams: J.W./Katz/Corbis Outline; Moby: Michael Wong/Corbis Outline; Apple: Joshua Kessler/Retna; Backstreet Boys: Andre Csillag; Luscious Jackson: Photograph by Anja Grabert; Orton: Rankin/Dazed & Confused/Camera Press/Retna. (**Internet**) AIBO: Photograph by Steve Freeman. OBITS Kubrick: Columbia Pictures/Archive Photos; Scott: Kobal Collection; Siskel: Donald Smetzer/Shooting Star; Plato: NBC/Globe Photos; Kelley: Michael Ochs Archives; Strickland, Strasberg: Archive Photos; Puzo: Bernard Gotfryd/Archive Photos; Hall: SMP/Globe Photos; Mature: Lester Glassner Collection/Neal Peters; DiMaggio: Neal Peters Collection; Springfield: Vivienne/CameraPress/Retna; Kahn: Edie Baskin/Corbis Outline; Funt: CBS Photo Archive; Bogarde: Bob Willoughby/MPTV; Reed: Popperfoto/Archive Photos; Corby: Yoram Kahana/Shooting Star; Crisp: Hans Verleur/Retna; Newley: Warner Bros./Archive Photos; Tormé, Sydney, Gould, Wences: Everett Collection.

ILLUSTRATIONS BY JOHN PIRMAN (DIVIDER PAGES) AND KIRSTEN ULVE (CARICATURES)